WORLD WAR II
IN PHOTOGRAPHS

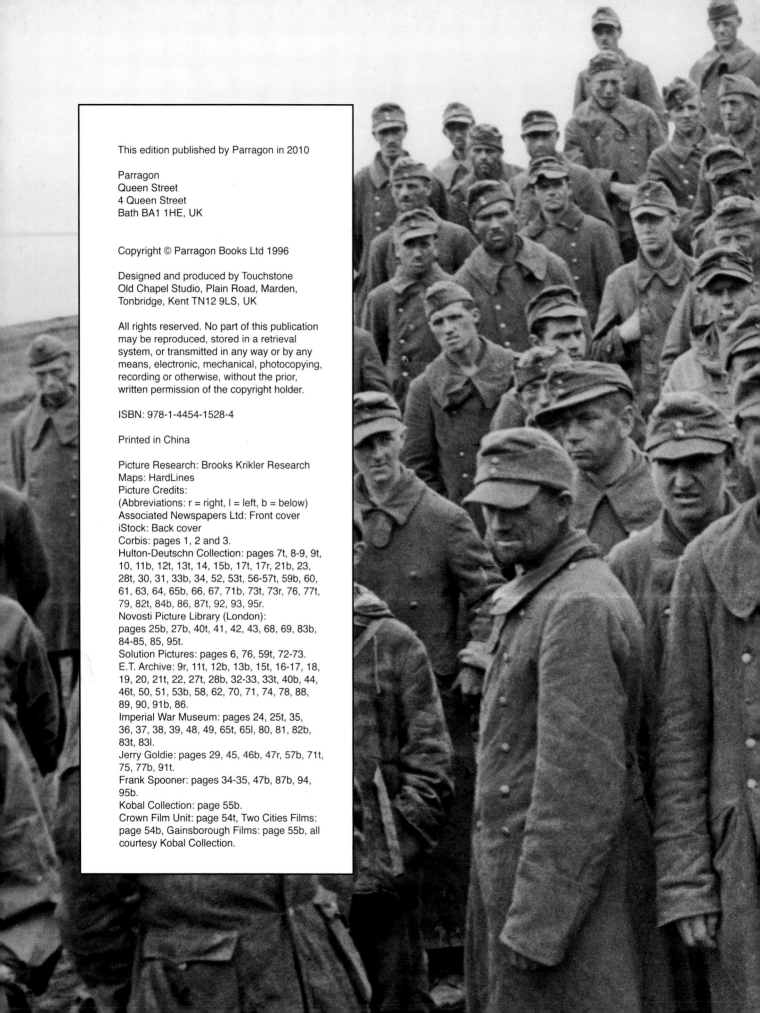

This edition published by Parragon in 2010

Parragon
Queen Street
4 Queen Street
Bath BA1 1HE, UK

Designed and produced by Touchstone
Old Chapel Studio, Plain Road, Marden,
Tonbridge, Kent TN12 9LS, UK

ISBN: 978-1-4454-1528-4

Printed in China

Picture Research: Brooks Krikler Research
Maps: HardLines
Picture Credits:
(Abbreviations: r = right, l = left, b = below)
Associated Newspapers Ltd: Front cover
iStock: Back cover
Corbis: pages 1, 2 and 3.
Hulton-Deutschn Collection: pages 7t, 8-9, 9t,
10, 11b, 12t, 13t, 14, 15b, 17t, 17r, 21b, 23,
28t, 30, 31, 33b, 34, 52, 53t, 56-57t, 59b, 60,
61, 63, 64, 65b, 66, 67, 71b, 73t, 73r, 76, 77t,
79, 82t, 84b, 86, 87t, 92, 93, 95r.
Novosti Picture Library (London):
pages 25b, 27b, 40t, 41, 42, 43, 68, 69, 83b,
84-85, 85, 95t.
Solution Pictures: pages 6, 76, 59t, 72-73.
E.T. Archive: 9r, 11t, 12b, 13b, 15t, 16-17, 18,
19, 20, 21t, 22, 27t, 28b, 32-33, 33t, 40b, 44,
46t, 50, 51, 53b, 58, 62, 70, 71, 74, 78, 88,
89, 90, 91b, 86.
Imperial War Museum: pages 24, 25t, 35,
36, 37, 38, 39, 48, 49, 65t, 65l, 80, 81, 82b,
83t, 83l.
Jerry Goldie: pages 29, 45, 46b, 47r, 57b, 71t,
75, 77b, 91t.
Frank Spooner: pages 34-35, 47b, 87b, 94,
95b.
Kobal Collection: page 55b.
Crown Film Unit: page 54t, Two Cities Films:
page 54b, Gainsborough Films: page 55b, all
courtesy Kobal Collection.

WORLD WAR II
IN PHOTOGRAPHS

ROBIN CROSS

PaRragon

Bath • New York • Singapore • Hong Kong • Cologne • Delhi • Melbourne

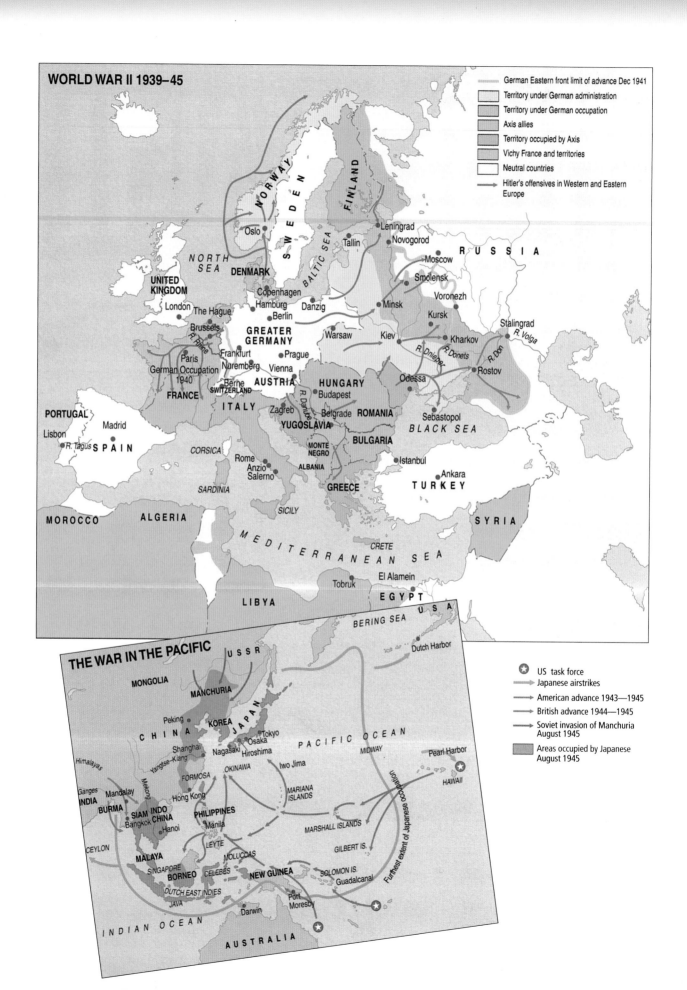

WORLD WAR II 1939–45

German Eastern front limit of advance Dec 1941
Territory under German administration
Territory under German occupation
Axis allies
Territory occupied by Axis
Vichy France and territories
Neutral countries
Hitler's offensives in Western and Eastern Europe

NORWAY
SWEDEN
FINLAND
Oslo
NORTH SEA
DENMARK
Tallin
Leningrad
Novogorod
RUSSIA
Moscow
Smolensk
UNITED KINGDOM
London
The Hague
Brussels
R. Rhine
Copenhagen
Hamburg
Berlin
Danzig
BALTIC SEA
Minsk
Voronezh
Kursk
Stalingrad
GREATER GERMANY
Warsaw
Kiev
Kharkov
R. Volga
Paris
Frankfurt
Prague
R. Dnieper
R. Donets
R. Don
German Occupation 1940
Nuremberg
Vienna
Rostov
FRANCE
Berne
SWITZERLAND
AUSTRIA
HUNGARY
Budapest
Odessa
PORTUGAL
Madrid
ITALY
Zagreb
R. Danube
Belgrade
ROMANIA
Sebastopol
BLACK SEA
Lisbon
R. Tagus
S P A I N
CORSICA
YUGOSLAVIA
MONTE NEGRO
BULGARIA
Istanbul
Ankara
Rome
Anzio
Salerno
ALBANIA
GREECE
TURKEY
SARDINIA
SICILY
CRETE
M E D I T E R R A N E A N   S E A
MOROCCO
ALGERIA
Tobruk
El Alamein
SYRIA
LIBYA
EGYPT

THE WAR IN THE PACIFIC

BERING SEA
USA
Dutch Harbor
USSR
MONGOLIA
MANCHURIA
US task force
Japanese airstrikes
American advance 1943—1945
British advance 1944—1945
Soviet invasion of Manchuria August 1945
Areas occupied by Japanese August 1945

Peking
KOREA
JAPAN
Tokyo
CHINA
Shanghai
Osaka
PACIFIC OCEAN
Yangtse-Kiang
Nagasaki
Hiroshima
MIDWAY
Pearl Harbor
Himalayas
FORMOSA
OKINAWA
Iwo Jima
HAWAII
Ganges
Mandalay
Hong Kong
MARIANA ISLANDS
INDIA
Mekong
BURMA
SIAM INDO CHINA
Bangkok
Hanoi
PHILIPPINES
Manila
MARSHALL ISLANDS
CEYLON
LEYTE
GILBERT IS.
MALAYA
MOLUCCAS
SINGAPORE
BORNEO
CELEBES
NEW GUINEA
SOLOMON IS.
Guadalcanal
Furthest extent of Japanese occupation
DUTCH EAST INDIES
JAVA
Port Moresby
Darwin
INDIAN OCEAN
AUSTRALIA

CONTENTS

THE ROAD TO WAR 1

THE SECOND World War was the last great battle of the war of 1914-18. The manner of Germany's defeat in 1918, with its army still in the field, and the reparations and territorial losses imposed by the Treaty of Versailles, left a permanent legacy of bitterness. Agitators like the ex-soldier Adolf Hitler, leader of the nascent Nazi Party, fed on these feelings of betrayal. Hitler's opinion of the Versailles settlement was simple: *'Only fools, liars and criminals could hope for mercy from the enemy . . . hatred grew in me, hatred for those responsible for the dead.'* His political career was to be devoted to the overturning of the Treaty of Versailles and the restoration of Germany as a world power.

After the failure of his Munich putsch in November 1923 and subsequent imprisonment, Hitler pursued a constitutional path to power, becoming German Chancellor in January 1933. A year later he announced that henceforth he would be German Head of State and Commander-in-Chief of the armed forces, binding them to him with an oath of allegiance.

Below: A disabled veteran of the trenches begs in a Berlin street in 1923, the year in which Adolf Hitler launched his unsuccessful coup in Munich. In the immediate postwar years Germany was wracked by bitter disillusion, raging inflation and pitched street battles between the private armies of the Communists and the extreme right.

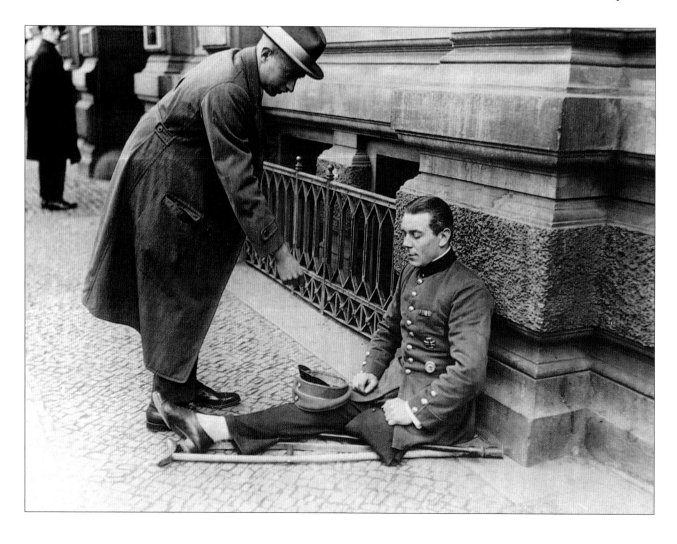

The impressive German economic recovery of the 1930s — achieved by a bold policy of deficit financing — underwrote Hitler's policy of rearmament, at first undertaken secretly and then announced to the world on 16 March 1935. Skilful propaganda concealed the underlying weakness of Germany's rapidly expanding armed forces, and their strength was constantly overestimated abroad.

Below: A truck full of troops trundles through Berlin's Potsdamer Platz during the Kapp putsch of March 1920. This attempt to seize power from Germany's Weimar Republic was supported by a significant section of the Army. It was during this period of chronic political and economic instability that Adolf Hitler emerged as the leader of the National Socialist German Workers' Party — the Nazi Party.

Right: The eyes have it. Adolf Hitler, ill at ease in a lounge suit, hones his spellbinding style with the help of his personal photographer Heinrich Hoffman, an earthy Bavarian who became the unofficial jester at the Nazi court.

THE ROAD TO WAR 2

W AR, OR rather the threat of it, was the driving force behind Hitler's foreign policy in the 1930s. He played brilliantly on the popular desire for peace in France and Britain, their governments' fear of a bloodletting even more terrible than that of 1914-18, and their inability to ally with the Soviet Union.

In March 1936 he reoccupied the demilitarized Rhineland, against the advice of his senior commanders. Britain and France failed to react, and Hitler embarked on an increasingly aggressive foreign policy. 'Volunteers' and much material went to General Franco's Nationalist forces in Spain for combat testing in the Spanish Civil War. In March 1938 Hitler annexed Austria. Czechoslovakia was next on his list. In September 1938 he outmanoeuvred the British and French at Godesberg and Munich to seize control of the Sudetenland and its ethnic German population. In March 1939 he swallowed up the rest of Czechoslovakia.

Below: The entry of the colours at the annual Nazi Party rally at Nuremberg, held every year in September. The Rally combined impressive demonstrations of growing German military might with the acutely skilful manipulation of mass emotion. In the vast perspectives of the Nuremberg stadium, which hosted the 1936 Olympic Games, thousands of perfectly drilled formations, flypasts of warplanes, torchlit processions and domed searchlights conveyed an overwhelming impression of national power, unity and purpose.

Left: Be prepared. A nightmarish vision of the future in which British Post Office workers take part in a 1937 anti-gas exercise. During the crisis over Czechoslovakia in 1938, 38 million gas mask were issued to men, women and children in Britain. In the late 1930s fears about the use of gas were justified. In 1935 The Italian dictator Benito Mussolini had used chemical weapons in his conquest of Ethiopia.

In the same month the Lithuanian port of Memel, with its large German population, was ceded to Germany. Hitler then turned to the free port of Danzig and the Polish Corridor to the Baltic, which separated East Prussia from Germany proper. On 23 August he secured his eastern flank by signing a non-aggression pact with the Soviet Union. War was now only a few days away.

Right: The first of the few. The Royal Air Force's 19 Squadron shows off its new Supermarine Spitfire fighters in the summer of 1938. In the autumn of that year the RAF's Fighter Command mustered 573 obsolete biplanes and only 93 monoplane aircraft. By then the German air force, the Luftwaffe, had used the Spanish Civil War to combat test its new Me109 fighter, He111 bomber and Ju87 dive-bomber.

THE INVASION OF POLAND

BEFORE DAWN on 1 September the German air force, the Luftwaffe, began a bombardment of strategic points inside Poland. It was the prelude to the first full-scale demonstration of the speed and striking power of *Blitzkrieg* (Lightning War) tactics, developed in the 1930s and based on deep armoured thrusts supported by dive- and level-bombers.

Within two days the Luftwaffe had gained complete control of the air and the Polish cordon defences were splintered into unco-ordinated groups. The German plan involved a double pincer movement. The inner pincer (Fourth, Eighth and Tenth Armies) was to close on the Vistula near Warsaw, while the outer pincer (Third and Fourteenth Armies) was to meet on the River Bug at Brest Litovsk, 100 miles east of the Polish capital.

The Polish army was dispersed in seven concentrations along its borders, with little in reserve, inviting swift envelopment by the German Army Group South, attacking on Poland's western frontier, and Army Group North, striking south from Pomerania and East Prussia.

> ### STEPS TO WAR
> **20 August:** Polish Crisis breaks.
> **23 August:** Britain warns Germany that she will fulfil her guarantees to Poland if Poland is attacked. German-Soviet Non-Aggression Pact signed in Moscow. Secret protocol agrees to partition of Poland and Soviet occupation of Baltic states.
> **24 August:** British Parliament approves Emergency Powers Bill.
> **25 August:** Britain and Poland sign mutual assistance treaty.
> **31 August:** Hitler orders attack on Poland.
> **2 September:** Poland's allies Britain and France issue ultimatum to Germany.
> **3 September:** Britain and France declare war on Germany after ultimatum is ignored.

Above right: Day of the dive-bomber. Junkers Ju87 'Stukas' over Poland. Roaming at will over the battlefield, the Stukas played havoc with Polish infantry and cavalry columns. The aircraft's fearsome reputation as a battle-winner belied its relatively modest performance, with a top speed of about 260mph and a bombload of 1,100 pounds.

Right: Hitler takes the salute as the victorious German Army marches through the streets of Warsaw. The long Polish nightmare was about to begin. It was the German aim not merely to dominate the Poles but totally to destroy their national identity. Poland was to become a slave nation.

Above: Forcing the frontier. German troops dismantle a barrier on the Polish border on 1 September 1939. At dawn that day the first of about a million men — concentrated in 41 infantry and 14 armoured (panzer) divisions — began to pour into Poland. The Poles fielded as many infantry but had little armour.

The outer encirclement was completed on 14 September. Three days later Poland's fate was sealed when the Red Army invaded from the east. Warsaw surrendered on the 27th and the fortress city of Modlin fell on the following day. The last Polish resistance was overcome at Kock, south-east of Warsaw, on 5 October. Polish casualties totalled 66,000 dead, over 200,000 wounded and nearly 700,000 prisoners. German casualties were light — some 10,500 dead, and 30,300 wounded.

THE PHONEY WAR

THE SPEED of German operations in Poland had, in part, been prompted by Hitler's fear that the French might launch an offensive in the West. In the event, the French and their British allies obliged him by remaining wholly inert.

The 150,000 troops of the British Expeditionary Force (BEF) which had crossed to France, dug in on the Belgian border but saw no action. Visiting the front line, Prime Minister Neville Chamberlain asked querulously, *'The Germans don't want to attack, do they?'* The greater part of the French Army, some 43 divisions, sat passively in or behind the Maginot Line, the fortress system on its eastern frontier. In September they made a feeble demonstration in the Saar, advanced a few miles, occupied a few abandoned villages and then withdrew.

There was an air of unreality about the war. The Royal Air Force was dropping propaganda leaflets rather than bombs on Germany. The bitter winter weather of 1939-40 was a greater threat to aircrew than the enemy's air defences. In Britain the 'Phoney War', as it came to be known, seemed to be a conflict run by civil servants rather than soldiers. The sole beneficiary was Adolf Hitler. Untroubled by the blockade on which the Allies pinned their hopes, he regrouped after the victory in Poland and planned his spring offensive, which was to begin with the invasion of Norway and Denmark.

Left: The shield of France. One of the huge guns in the Maginot Line, the embodiment in steel and concrete of the trench systems of World War I. Named after the French war minister who initiated it, the Maginot Line was meant to deter aggression but spoke volumes for the defensive mentality of the French Army. The Line's fatal weakness was that it could be outflanked through neutral Belgium.

Left: Scramble! Pilots of the RAF's 87 Squadron, part of the British Expeditionary Force in France, race for their Hurricanes in March 1940. At the time of its introduction into service in the autumn of 1937 the Hawker Hurricane was the first operational fighter capable of exceeding 300mph and the first to be armed with eight machine guns.

Above: Dominoes and gas masks in a London family's Anderson shelter. A corrugated iron construction sunk into thousands of back gardens, the Anderson shelter was to save many lives during the Blitz. It was named after Sir John Anderson, the British Home Secretary, 1939-40, a firm advocate of its use. Remembering nights in the Anderson shelter, the historian Norman Longmate wrote, 'To be inside an Anderson shelter felt rather like being entombed in a small, dark bicycle shed, smelling of earth and damp'.

Right: End of an ocean raider. The German pocket battleship Graf Spee ablaze in the River Plate off Montevideo, Uruguay, where she had taken refuge after a running battle with a British cruiser squadron. Rather than expose her to destruction by the heavier Royal Navy units steaming towards the Plate, Hitler ordered Graf Spee to be scuttled on 17 December 1939. Three days later her commander, Captain Hans Langsdorff, committed suicide.

er as a
y and
eatened the
n-ore from
ay.
ly
s later
g troop
d,
sing the

Below: Bombs fall on the Norwegian port of Narvik. The Germans occupied the town on 9 April 1940. A week later the British and French landed a force in the area but Narvik did not fall to the Allies until the end of May. In two naval battles fought off Narvik in April, the Royal Navy destroyed half the complement of the German Navy's destroyers. Shortage of destroyers was to play a significant part in forestalling the German invasion of southern England in the summer of 1940.

Above: German infantry advance behind armoured cover through a clutter of bicycles. The skies above them were dominated by the Luftwaffe, which made life for the Allied troops extremely uncomfortable.

Right: The occupiers arrive. German troops disembark in Oslo in May 1940. In April the former war minister, Vidkun Quisling, whose name later became synonymous with treachery, proclaimed himself premier of a pro-German government, but real power lay with the German Reich Commissioner, Josef Terboven, who reported directly to Hitler. Norway's legitimate government and King Haakon VII had fled to London.

Only at Oslo, the Norwegian capital, did the Germans encounter serious resistance. The cruiser *Blücher* was sunk and the battleship *Lutzow* damaged before airborne troops captured the city. Denmark was overrun on 9 April.

Between 10 and 13 April the Royal Navy inflicted heavy damage on the German naval force ferrying troops to Narvik, and five days later the Allies landed near Narvik. Over the next three days they also landed north and south of Trondheim, but these footholds were eliminated by the Germans as they swept inland, and evacuations followed at the beginning of May. An Allied force captured Narvik on 28 May but was also forced to evacuate on June 8-9 because of events in France. In the withdrawal the carrier *Glorious* was sunk and the German battlecruisers *Scharnhorst* and *Gneisenau* were badly damaged.

THE FALL OF FRANCE

O N 10 MAY, the day Winston Churchill became British Prime Minister, Germany attacked Holland and Belgium, catching the British and French deployed in three army groups behind the French frontier.

The British and French high commands had expected the major German thrust to be directed through the Low Countries, as it had been in 1914, and indeed this was the original German intention. But the plan had been changed, and maximum pressure was now applied not in the north but through the heavily wooded Ardennes, which the Allies had thought impenetrable by tanks. France's supposedly impregnable Maginot Line was simply outflanked.

By 14 May, German tanks had crossed the Meuse at Sedan and were sweeping north to trap huge numbers of French and British troops in northern France and Belgium. German armour reached the English Channel on the 20th, and a week later the BEF, which had fallen back on the Channel ports, began its evacuations from Dunkirk. When Operation Dynamo ended on 4 June, some 338,000 troops (225,000 of them British) had been taken off the beaches. The next day the Germans began mopping up remaining French resistance. An armistice was signed on the 22nd, and four days later fighting ceased. Italy had declared war on Britain and France on 10 June.

Right: A Ju87 of the crack 'Immelmann' wing is prepared for take-off. Although the Stuka terrorized raw French troops during the Battle of France, its weaknesses were also exposed, notably its vulnerability when pulling out of a steep dive. It was withdrawn from the Battle of Britain in mid-August 1940, after suffering heavy losses at the hands of Fighter Command. Later in the war the Stuka was adapted to an anti-shipping role and performed sterling service on the Eastern Front as a heavily armed 'tank-buster'.

Left: British infantry under attack from the air as they await evacuation from the Dunkirk pocket. The destruction of the trapped Allied troops had been entrusted to the Luftwaffe by Hitler, who was preoccupied with the elimination of the remaining French armies south of the Somme and still fearful of an Allied counterstroke against his armour in an area cut by canals and threatend with flooding. The Luftwaffe failed in its task. In furious air battles over Dunkirk it lost 156 aircraft and the RAF 106.

Above: No other tourist has paid his first visit to Paris as a conqueror. Hitler inspects the Eiffel Tower at the end of June 1940. Walking on his right is the architect Albert Speer, who in 1942 became Hitler's highly capable Armaments Minister.

THE BATTLE OF BRITAIN

THE FALL of France had brought the seemingly invincible German army to the coast of France. Adolf Hitler brooded over the invasion of southern England, codenamed *Sealion*, an operation for which neither he nor his high command had any real enthusiasm.

The success of *Sealion* depended on the destruction by the Luftwaffe of the Royal Air Force's Fighter Command. The air battle began in earnest on 10 July 1940, and for three weeks the Luftwaffe and Fighter Command exchanged opening blows, probing each other's strengths and weaknesses.

The battle moved into a higher gear in August, and on 15 August the Luftwaffe launched its main attack, codenamed *Adler* (Eagle), to provoke and win a decisive battle against Fighter Command. In fierce air fighting the Luftwaffe lost 72 aircraft on what became known as 'Black Thursday'.

RAF losses, which were now outstripping the supply of new aircraft, were also causing concern. Exhaustion had set in among the battered squadrons defending the key battleground over south-east England. Several of Fighter Command's vital sector stations lay in ruins, although they were still flying off aircraft.

Throughout the battle, the Luftwaffe had fatally switched back and forth between targets — the RAF's coastal radar installations, Fighter Command's sector stations, aircraft factories — without knocking out any of them. On 7 September it launched its first mass daylight raid on London. The Luftwaffe believed that the RAF had only 100 aircraft left, but on 15 September it suffered a crushing defeat when two heavily escorted waves of bombers ran into nearly 300 British fighters in the skies over London. Air superiority had been decisively denied to the Luftwaffe, and on 12 October Hitler ordered the indefinite postponement of *Sealion*.

Below: Ready to roll. A Messerschmitt Me 109 fighter of 1/JG2 Richthofen taxis for take-off. The Me109 and the Spitfire were evenly matched but the former was hampered by its combat range of 125 miles, which limited it to a maximum of 30 minutes over southern England. A Luftwaffe commander later complained: 'The German fighters found themselves in a similar predicament to a dog on a chain which wants to attack a foe but cannot harm him because of his limited orbit'.

Right: Two Hurricanes of 501 Squadron scramble from Gravesend on 15 August at the height of the battle. Although less glamorous than the legendary Spitfire, the rugged Hurricane bore the brunt of the fighting in the Battle of Britain from July to November 1940. The top-scoring Fighter Command squadron of the Battle, 303, flew Hurricanes and is credited with 126½ confirmed victories.

Above: An armourer, one of the many unsung heroes of the Battle of Britain, readies a Spitfire for combat. Each aircraft had a ground crew of three — a rigger, fitter and armourer. The squadrons of Fighter Command were sustained by a long chain stretching back from the ground crews to the workers in aircraft factories.

Below: Luftwaffe aircrew are marched away from the burning wreckage of their He111. The speed of the twin-engined He111 was no guarantee of safety from Spitfires and Hurricanes, and a feature of the Battle of Britain was the high proportion of bombers which returned to their bases with dead and severely wounded crew.

THE BLITZ

O N SATURDAY 7 September 1940 the Luftwaffe launched its first attack on London. That afternoon its commander-in-chief, Reichsmarschall Hermann Göring, stood on the clifftop at Cap Gris Nez watching flights of bombers thundering overhead across the Channel. The Blitz was about to begin.

That day 300 aircraft dropped more than 300 tons of bombs on London's docks and the densely packed streets of the East End. The fires they started lit the way for 250 more bombers which attacked between 8pm and dawn. To a fire officer battling the blaze in the Surrey docks it seemed that *'the whole bloody world's on fire!'*

For the next 56 nights London was bombed from dusk to dawn, the bombers following the silver line of the Thames to strike at the biggest target in the world. By the end of the year the death toll in London had reached 13,600, with many thousands more injured and over 250,000 people left homeless. The cost to the Luftwaffe was negligible; anti-aircraft guns were downing only one enemy aircraft in every 300.

In the 1930s British planners calculated that civilian morale would crack almost as soon as the bombs started to fall. But as the weeks passed, people found that life was bearable in spite of the bombs. London proved too tough a nut to crack, and the Luftwaffe turned its attention to ports like Southampton and industrial centres in the Midlands. On 14 November the city of Coventry suffered a devastating raid which introduced a new word to the language – to 'Coventrate'.

The final phase of the Blitz began on 16 April 1941, climaxing with a huge raid on London on 10 May which left one-third of the capital's streets impassable and 160,000 families without water, gas and electricity. But by the end of June 1941 two-thirds of the Luftwaffe had been transferred to the Eastern Front. The Blitz was over.

Above: A Heinkel HeIII drones over the East End of London. This dramatic photograph was distributed in Germany to suggest how vulnerable the capital of the British Empire was to Hitler's bombers. But by switching the attack to London on 8 September, partly in response to an RAF bombing raid on Berlin, Hitler threw away all chance of winning the Battle of Britain.

Right: A tin-hatted Air Raid Warden takes tea in his post, the lynchpin at a local level of Britain's civil defence system. Each post was supposed to control an area containing about 500 people. In London there were about ten posts a square mile. In 1939 there were 1.5 million civil defence personnel, over two-thirds of them volunteers.

Left: Spirit of the Blitz. In April 1941 Winston Churchill declared: 'I see the damage done by the enemy attacks; but I also see, side by side with the devastation and the ruins, quiet, confident, bright and smiling eyes, beaming with the consciousness of being associated with a cause far higher and wider than any human or personal issue. I can see the spirit of an unquenchable people'.

Right: Londoners take refuge from the bombs on the platform of the Elephant and Castle Underground station. At the height of the Blitz about 170,000 people sheltered in the Tube every night. Legend has it that their snoring rose and fell like a wind.

BALKAN INTERLUDE

SMARTING AT Hitler's success in the West, the Italian dictator Benito Mussolini invaded Albania and Greece in October 1940. He soon ran into trouble, was driven back into Albania by the Greeks and had to be rescued by his German ally.

Hitler also wanted to protect his southern flank before launching the long-planned invasion of the Soviet Union. When the pro-German Prince Paul of Yugoslavia was overthrown in a coup encouraged by the movement of 60,000 British troops to Greece, Hitler went on the offensive.

In Operation Punishment, which began on 6 April 1941, the Germans overran Yugoslavia in only ten days. The conquest of Greece took just over two weeks. The British evacuated some 18,000 of the troops in Greece to the island of Crete, which was captured by the Germans at the end of May after an airborne invasion. Nine British warships were sunk and 17 seriously damaged in a second evacuation.

The German victory in Crete was gained at the cost of nearly 10,000 casualties. Horrified at the losses, Hitler cancelled a proposed airborne seizure of Malta.

Right: The swastika is run aloft on the Parthenon in Athens. The campaigns in Greece and Yugoslavia cost the German Army barely 5,000 casualties. In Yugoslavia the Germans took 345,000 prisoners. Greek losses amounted to 70,000 killed or wounded and 270,000 captured. The British sustained 12,000 casualties in the Greek campaign and lost all their heavy equipment.

Right: A German transport aircraft goes down as parachutes fill the skies over north-west Crete on 20 May 1941. In the desperate fighting which followed the drops, the paratroops suffered heavy casualties, but their seizure of Maleme airfield gave them a foothold for airborne reinforcement which ensured victory.

Below: The British warship *Kipling* steams into Alexandria harbour after the fall of Crete. Waving to the shore from the bridge is the flamboyant Lord Mountbatten, commander of the Fifth Destroyer Flotilla, whose ship, the destroyer *Kelly*, had been sunk by Stukas during the British evacuation. Mountbatten and the survivors from *Kelly* were picked up by *Kipling*, which was also attacked and damaged by German aircraft. Mountbatten was later appointed Chief of Combined Operations before becoming Supreme Allied Commander, South-East Asia.

BARBAROSSA 1

AT 3.30am on Sunday 22 June 1941, the day after the 129th anniversary of Napoleon's attack on Russia in 1812, seven German infantry armies, their advance spearheaded by four panzer groups, invaded the Soviet Union. The codename for the operation was Barbarossa.

Three million German soldiers, supported by 3,580 tanks, 7,184 guns and nearly 2,000 aircraft were on the move along a front of 2,000 miles. The Red Army, in the middle of a wholesale reorganization and deployed forward to cover every curve and crevice in its frontiers, was caught in a series of massive encirclements. At Minsk and Smolensk in July, the Germans took 400,000 prisoners. In September, 600,000 went into the bag, trapped in the wide bend of the Dnieper.

Below: Armoured drive. A MkIII panzer and panzer grenadiers advance across a cornfield in the fierce heat of the Russian summer. The MkIII was the backbone of the panzer divisions in the early stages of the German campaign in Russia, but was to meet its match in the Russian T-34, the best all-round tank of the war, which was introduced in 1941.

Two months of victory exacted their price. Battle deaths, wounds and sickness struck half a million men from the German order of battle. On 11 July the commander of 18th Panzer Division expressed fears that the loss of men and equipment would prove insupportable '*if we do not intend to win ourselves to death*'.

Right: House to house fighting in Rostov, a major rail junction in southern Russia close to the Sea of Azov. The city fell to the German First Panzer Army on 21 November 1941, but was retaken by the Russians a week later after a fierce counterattack. It was the first serious setback for the Germans in Barbarossa and led to the resignation of the commander of Army Group South, Field Marshal von Rundstedt.

Below: A column of refugees in the Ukraine, with the smoke of battle rising behind them. Often described as the granary of Russia, the Ukraine was the objective of Army Group South in Barbarossa.

BARBAROSSA 2

ARLY IN October 1941 the depleted German Army Group North laid siege to Leningrad. But by now Russia's vast spaces, primitive roads and gruelling climate were taking their toll on the German Army.

Scorching summer heat gave way to seas of autumn mud. In October the first snows of winter began to fall. Hitler was now caught between driving straight for Moscow or reinforcing his extended southern flank to secure the raw materials and agricultural riches of the Ukraine. Winter — for which the German high command had not equipped its army — arrived while the Führer was still shuttling forces up and down his battlefront.

Below: The people of Moscow dig anti-tank ditches on the approaches to the Russian capital in the autumn of 1941. The setbacks of the opening phase of Barbarossa encouraged the Soviet dictator, Josef Stalin, to transform the struggle against Germany into the 'Great Patriotic War'. The Orthodox Church was enlisted in the war effort and 'Mother Russia' rather than the Communist Party invoked as a rallying cry.

Right: German motor transport trapped in the glutinous mud of the 1942 spring thaw. Russian winter cold was a quick killer but the endless seas of autumn and spring mud destroyed mobility and sapped morale. On Russia's primitive roads twelve hours of rain was enough to reduce a main highway to an impassable morass. In these conditions, horsed transport came into its own. For all their vaunted Panzer spearheads, the German Army in Russia depended on horses for over 80 per cent of its motive power.

The German advance slowed amid blizzards and temperatures so low that they welded artillery pieces into immovable blocks on the rock-hard earth. Some German patrols reached a tram terminus on the outskirts of Moscow. They could see the domes of the Kremlin glinting in the sun. On 6 December the Russians counter-attacked with fresh and well-equipped divisions rushed from Siberia. They drove the German Army Group Centre back 200 miles before the offensive slithered to a halt in the glutinous mud of the spring thaw of 1942. *Blitzkrieg* had met its match.

Below: The retreat from Moscow. The German Army was ill-equipped for the rigours of the Russian winter. In the battle for Moscow the German Fourth Army's losses to frotsbite were more than twice its battle casualties.

THE BATTLE OF THE ATLANTIC

WINSTON Churchill considered that the Battle of the Atlantic was the *'dominating factor all through the war. Never could we forget that everything depended on its outcome'.* If Britain's trans-Atlantic supply line with America had been cut by the German Navy's U-boats, the British would have been unable to continue the war. The battle to defeat the submarine threat was the longest and most important fought by the British.

At first the U-boats gained the upper hand. Hunting in groups known as 'wolfpacks' and guided to their targets by long-range reconnaissance aircraft, the U-boats could stay at sea for long periods, refuelled by supply submarines. By co-ordinating surface attacks at night, they could overwhelm convoy escorts by sheer weight of numbers.

Crisis point was reached at the beginning of 1943. The U-boats were sinking ships at twice the rate they were being built, while for every U-boat sunk, two were launched. The U-boats seemed to have victory within their grasp.

Opposite: The last photograph of the British battlecruiser *Hood* as she went into action against the German pocket battleship *Bismarck*, south of Greenland, on 24 May 1941. *Hood* was sunk by plunging fire from *Bismarck*, which also damaged the battleship *Prince of Wales*, from which the photograph was taken. *Bismarck's* triumph was shortlived. She was crippled by a torpedo, dropped by a Swordfish torpedo-bomber from the carrier *Ark Royal* and on 27 May was overhauled and pounded to bits by the battleships *Rodney* and *King George V*. The 'coup de grâce' was delivered by a torpedo fired by the cruiser *Dorsetshire*. Only 107 of *Bismarck's* crew survived.

Technology turned the tide. Powerful new centimetric radars were fitted to long-range Allied aircraft equipped with searchlights and depth charges, enabling them to hunt the U-boats at night. High Frequency Direction Finding (known as 'Huff Duff') helped convoy escorts to pinpoint and shadow U-boats when they were transmitting back to base. Hunter-killer groups built around fast escort carriers took a heavy toll of U-boats.

By the summer of 1943 the tonnage of Allied shipping launched overtook that lost to the U-boats for the first time in the war. The U-boat menace had been mastered. The Germans' own technological innovations, the endurance-improving Schnorkel tube and the ocean-going Type XXI, ancestor of all modern submarines, proved too little and too late to regain the initiative.

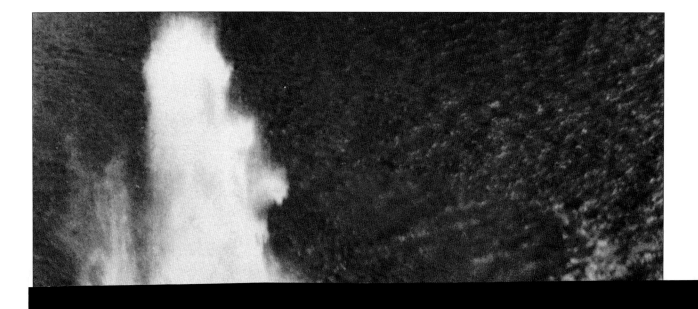

KEEP SMILING THROUGH: THE BRITISH HOME FRONT

NO NATION mobilized more thoroughly for war than the British. *'Don't you know there's a war on?'* were the words which rang through the conflict, from rationing queues to shell factories.

Peacetime staples quickly became luxuries. Meat rationing was introduced in March 1940, shrinking as ships went down in the Atlantic. In bad times the weekly butter ration of four ounces was halved and the cheese allowance came to resemble mousetrap bait, in size as well as quality. Nevertheless, fair shares for all meant that the diet and health of the nation improved during the war.

Below: Arrivals and departures. Troops and evacuees at a London railway station. At the beginning of the war about 1.5 million children were evacuated from Britain's cities to 'reception areas' safe from German bombs. When the bombs failed to materialize, many returned to their homes. The onset of the Blitz in September 1940 prompted a new wave of evacuation. Evacuation and the imposition of the black-out were the two main features of life on the home front during the Phoney War.

Right: The Army that never fought. A Home Guard sentry keeps watch outside London's County Hall in the summer of 1940, when a German invasion seemed imminent. Originally called the Local Defence Volunteers, the Home Guard was formed in May 1940 and by the end of June numbered some 1.5 ill-equipped but enthusiastic men. Hitler called them a 'murder band', but 'Dad's Army' had the last laugh.

The entire nation was embraced by the war effort and a substantial civilian part of it was propelled into the front line by the Blitz. In the winter of 1940 a woman Air Raid Warden in the East End was in greater physical danger every night than the majority of men serving in the forces.

The conscription of women began in December 1941. By mid-1943 nine out of ten single women were in the forces or war industry, serving as Land Girls, operating mixed anti-aircraft batteries or working as welders in Britain's shipyards. Margaret Weldon, a member of the Women's Auxiliary Air Force (WAAF) recalled: *'In a way it was like going to university. We were mostly that age and you see people change as they grow up through a war. Before the war I had never been anywhere much and I knew very little. The people I knew were confined to my local area. In the WAAF I met all kinds of people in all kinds of circumstances. I saw things I never thought I would see. And there's an instant bond between us all when we meet again today'.*

Below: A woman at work in a munitions factory. Women were quick to fill the places vacated by men serving in the forces. In the shipyards they became expert welders, particularly adept at intricate work requiring finesse and attention to detail. Even so, they were still paid less than their male colleagues.

Below: Harvest time for members of the Women's Land Army. Eventually there were some 80,000 Land Girls boosting agricultural output. About 1,000 of them worked as rat catchers. Another 6,000 joined the Timber Corps, selecting and felling trees in remote parts of the countryside and working in sawmills.

RISING SUN: JAPAN'S ROAD TO WAR

JAPAN HAD begun to intervene in mainland China in 1931, when the troops it stationed there to guard the Japanese-run railways in Manchuria took over the province. War with China followed in 1937 when the Japanese garrison guarding the embassy at Peking exchanged fire with Chinese troops before going on to the offensive.

Japan went on to occupy the entire Chinese coast and large tracts of the interior. Without military support from Britain, which allowed war materials to be transported along the 'Burma Road' to Chungking, the Chinese government, headed by Chiang Kai-shek, would have been unable to resist the Japanese.

The United States had stood aside from the Japanese expansion. But in September 1940 it was extended to French Indochina, where Vichy France granted Japan military bases from which it could threaten Malaya, the East Indies and the US protectorate of the Philippines.

President Roosevelt chose an economic weapon to halt the Japanese advance, imposing an embargo on rubber, which was followed in July 1941 by the freezing of all Japanese assets in the United States and the announcement of an oil embargo against all aggressors, including Japan. At a stroke the Japanese were deprived of 90 per cent of their oil supplies and 75 per cent of their foreign trade. The Japanese were confronted with a choice – diplomatic retreat from their Chinese conquests or war. They decided to play for time while planning a surprise attack on the US Navy.

Below: War baby. A child abandoned in the ruins of Shanghai after a Japanese air raid. The city fell to the Japanese on 8 November 1937.

Above: The battleship *Yamato*, symbol of Japanese naval might. Designed to outgun any battleship afloat, with nine 18-inch guns, the *Yamato* and her sister ship *Musashi* entered service in 1940 at a time when the aircraft carrier was becoming the capital ship of the world's naval powers. *Yamato* was sunk on 7 April 1945 by American carrier-borne aircraft while sailing on a suicide mission against the US forces invading Okinawa.

Below: Chinese civilians are executed by Japanese troops in 1937. The Japanese invasion of China and subsequent conquest of swathes of the Pacific and South-East Asia was characterized by extremes of brutality.

PEARL HARBOR: DAY OF INFAMY

AFTER THE imposition of the American oil embargo, Admiral Osami Nagano, Chief of the Japanese General Staff, observed that Japan was like 'a *fish in a pond from which the water is gradually being drained away'*.

Alternative sources of raw materials were relatively near at hand, in Borneo, Java and Sumatra, Malaya and Burma. The only way to obtain them would be to undertake the rapid military conquest of a vast area of the Far East. In November 1941 talks began in Washington with the aim of averting hostilities. Meanwhile the Japanese prepared a surprise carrier strike against the US Pacific Fleet's base at Pearl Harbor on the Hawaiian island of Oahu.

Above: The destroyer *Shaw* explodes in its dry dock after a direct hit during the Japanese attack on Pearl Harbor, 7 December 1941. Shortly before 1pm on the 8th, President Roosevelt asked Congress to declare war against Japan. Britain declared war on Japan the same day. Three days later Germany and Italy — honouring treaty obligations with Japan — declared war on the United States. The British Prime Minister Winston Churchill recognized this as the turning point in the war. With the vast military potential of United States engaged against Japan *and* Germany, Churchill was convinced that the war would be won.

On 26 November the Japanese fleet left harbour. Maintaining radio silence, and under cover of clouds and squalls, it sailed to its attack positions 200 miles from Pearl Harbor. The Americans were aware of Japanese intentions; they had been decoding and reading Japanese messages for months. But they were ignorant of Japan's precise plans.

At 7.55am on 7 December the Japanese struck, achieving complete surprise. Aircraft from six carriers sank or disabled six of the battleships anchored at Pearl Harbor and destroyed over 300 aircraft on the ground. One vital factor cheated them of annihilating victory; the Pacific Fleet's two carriers were on a training cruise and escaped attack.

Below: A Japanese airman's view of 'Battleship Row' at Pearl Harbor. Of the seven battleships sunk or damaged during the raid, only two, *Arizona* and *Oklahoma*, would never sail again. *Pennsylvania*, in dry dock, escaped serious damage. Crucially, the second wave of Japanese warplanes failed to attack Pearl Harbor's dock repair and oil storage facilities, the destruction of which would have immobilized the US Pacific Fleet.

NORTH AFRICAN SEESAW 1

FOR THREE years after the fall of France, the only theatre in which the ground forces of the Western Allies were able to come to grips with the Axis was in North Africa. Commanders in the Western Desert of Egypt and Libya were as much prisoners of geography and climate as their counterparts on the Eastern Front.

The Western Desert was an arid waste yielding nothing. Over long stretches, the landward edge of the coastal plain was bounded by high ground or a steep depression which confined the movement of armies to a narrow 40-mile strip. The war in North Africa was characterized by a series of advances and retreats along this 1,200-mile-long strip, stretching from Tripoli in the west to Alexandria in the east, along which a chain of small ports were the only points of military value. The war took the form of dashes from one point of maritime supply to the next, with the aim of depriving the enemy of water, fuel, ammunition, food and reinforcements which, in that order, were the essentials of desert warfare.

The desert might seem a clean environment, but it was a cruel one for the men who fought in it. They endured broiling heat and freezing nights, flies and grit, sweat-soaked clothing and desert sores. A shower of rain could turn sand into the consistency of mud as deep and clinging as any on the Eastern Front.

Below: An Afrika Korps MkIII panzer drives through the desert during Rommel's drive to Bir Hacheim in June 1942. Its British counterpart, the Matilda infantry tank, could not compete with the MkIII and was withdrawn as a gun tank at the end of 1942. The MkIII encountered more serious opposition with the arrival in North Africa in May 1942 of the American M3 Grant tank, with its sponson-mounted 75mm gun which was capable of firing armour-piercing and high-explosive ammunition.

Left: Scourge of British armour, the German 88mm gun in action at Mersa el Brega in April 1941. An anti-aircraft gun developed by Krupp in the early 1930s, its capabilities as an anti-tank weapon were first noted during the Spanish Civil War.

Below: In a typically bleak desert landsape, littered with the detritus of war, British infantry bring in German and Italian prisoners captured in October 1942.

NORTH AFRICAN SEESAW 2

I N 1940 the British had things their own way in North Africa. Italy had declared war on Britain on 10 June 1940, and in September launched a ponderous offensive into Egypt from its North African colony in Libya. Although heavily outnumbered, the British fought a brilliant campaign to drive the Italians back 500 miles to Benghazi.

The situation underwent a rapid change in February 1941 with the arrival of the German Afrika Korps commanded by General Erwin Rommel. His brilliant handling of armour and tactic of drawing British tanks on to his formidable 88mm anti-tank guns made him a constant threat until, starved of supplies, he was bludgeoned into defeat by General Montgomery at the second Battle of El Alamein in November 1942.

Below: British infantry move forward at the second Battle of El Alamein, a bitter slogging match which was opened on 23 October 1942 by a massive bombardment from 800 British guns. The commander of the British Eighth Army, General Montgomery, enjoyed a big material advantage over his Axis opponents, and by the evening of 3 November had reduced the Afrika Korps to only 30 operational tanks. Shortly before dawn on 4 November Rommel began the long withdrawal to Tunisia.

Rommel's defeat was secured by the virtual throttling of the Axis supply lines across the Mediterranean and the quantitative superiority in material which the British Eighth Army was able to achieve by the autumn of 1942. Rommel's difficulties were exacerbated by the fact that, in Hitler's eyes, the North African theatre was always a sideshow. Nevertheless, it was not until May 1943 that the German and Italian forces in North Africa surrendered, a process hastened by the Allied landings in Morocco and Algeria in November 1942.

Below: A knocked-out German MkIII tank is captured on 29 October, a week into the second Battle of El Alamein, the decisive battle of the Desert War. The British victory was qualified by a slow pursuit of the retreating Germans, hampered by heavy rain, fuel shortages and Montgomery's characteristic caution.

Below: Desert raiders. Colonel David Stirling with one of his deep penetration raiding parties which operated far behind enemy lines in conjunction with units of the Long Range Desert Group. Stirling's creation evolved into the Special Air Service (SAS) Regiment. Stirling was captured in Tunisia in 1943 and, after many attempts to escape, finished the war in the confines of Colditz castle.

THE RED ARMY STRIKES BACK

IN THE summer of 1942 Hitler returned to business left unfinished in front of Moscow in December 1941. Once again the panzers rolled: Army Group A struck through the Donets corridor to Stalingrad while Army Group B drove through Rostov to the Caucasus and on towards the Soviet Union's southernmost oilfields at Baku on the Caspian Sea.

Below: A Red Army battalion commander leads his men into action. After its near destruction in 1941, a new battle-hardened Red Army emerged to wrest the initiative back from the Germans.

Below: German infantry pick their way warily through the ruins of Stalingrad. The soldier in the centre carries the base plate of a mortar and the man on the left a rack of bombs.

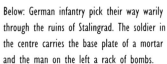

Above: The horror and the pity. The aftermath of a German atrocity in the Kerch peninsula in the Crimea captured by the great war photographer Dmitri Baltermants in 1942. Nazi ideology ensured that the war on the Eastern Front was fought with unequalled savagery. The Russians repaid their enemy in kind. By the end of 1944 there were few Red Army men who did not have a personal score to settle with the Germans.

Hitler's plan was unhinged by his growing obsession with the seizure of Stalingrad, the straggling industrial city on the banks of the Volga. Russian resistance denied him the prize and, by the winter of 1942, turned Stalingrad into a tomb for the encircled German Sixth Army. On 31 January 1943 its commander, Field Marshal Paulus, and 100,000 men went into captivity. A massive Soviet counter-attack, launched in January 1943 between Orel and Rostov, threatened Kharkov and the German forces withdrawing from the Caucasus.

The Soviet offensive was halted in its tracks by a brilliantly weighted counterblow delivered by Field Marshal von Manstein in February-March 1943. When the fighting died down in the mud of the spring thaw, it left a huge fist-shaped salient, centred around the city of Kursk, in the heartland of the Ukraine, jutting westward into the German line.

KURSK: CLASH OF ARMOUR

THE KURSK bulge exercised a horrible fascination on Hitler. He told General Guderian, Inspector of Armoured Troops, that every time he thought of the impending attack on the salient his stomach turned over.

The build-up for the operation, codenamed Citadel and aimed at clawing back the initiative after the surrender of Sixth Army at Stalingrad, took three months. The Red Army, reorganized, re-equipped and increasingly confident, had been warned of the German plans by the 'Lucy' spy network in Switzerland and agents placed in the British decoding centre at Bletchley Park (see p.80). Under the overall direction of Marshal Zhukov it prepared to defend the salient in massive strength and depth.

Below: Into the cauldron. T-34s of Fifth Guards Tank Army carry infantry into action in the Kursk salient while Illyushin Il-2 Shturmovik attack bombers flash across the sky ahead of them. Some 6,000 tanks and assault guns were drawn into the Battle of Kursk. Losses on both sides were about 1,500 armoured vehicles, but the Germans lacked the reserves to recover their strength. In contrast, Russian tank production capacity far exceeded Germany's.

When Hitler launched his tanks against the southern and northern shoulders of the Kursk salient on 5 July 1943, they were caught in the Soviet killing grounds and mangled beyond repair. No sooner had the German thrusts been contained than the Red Army delivered a series of crushing counter-attacks which by September had driven the German Army back to the line of the River Dnieper. Hitler had gambled all on the throw of a single dice and had lost the initiative on the Eastern Front, never to regain it.

Above: Red Army anti-tank riflemen under fire. No soldier was better equipped for anti-tank fighting than the Red Army infantryman. It suited his ability to hug the ground and defend his native soil to the last breath. By June 1943 the Russian infantry had received 1.5 million anti-tank rifles.

Left: The face of defeat. A German artilleryman in the Orel salient. Between July and October 1943 'irreplaceable' German losses on the Eastern Front reached 365,000, the greater part inflicted at Kursk and during the retreat to the Dnieper.

STRATEGIC BOMBING 1

I N 1940 the Luftwaffe's twin-engined bombers lacked the payload to level London and Britain's industrial cities. RAF Bomber Command was no better placed to win the war by bombing alone, the cherished hope of air strategists in the 1930s. Its aircraft groped their way blindly over a blacked-out Europe. Even on moonlit nights most of them were dropping their bombs miles from their targets.

Nevertheless, the bombing campaign remained the only way the British could strike directly at Germany. Things improved in 1942 with the arrival in numbers of four-engined bombers equipped with increasingly sophisticated radio navigation aids. This coincided with a change of policy. Although the destruction of precision targets remained an intermittent, and spectacular, feature of Bomber Command operations, most of the RAF's bombs would now fall on 'area' targets. If Bomber Command could not destroy German war factories, it could destroy the cities where the factory workers lived. Bomber Command's C-in-C, Air Chief Marshal Sir Arthur Harris, believed that the systematic destruction of Germany's cities would, by itself, bring an end to the war. All other targets, for example those linked with oil or fighter production, Harris dismissed as mere 'panaceas'.

Below: A Wellington bomber and crews of the RAF's 149 Squadron on their return from Bomber Command's raid on Berlin on 25 August 1940 which partly prompted Hitler to turn the Luftwaffe against London. Designed by Barnes Wallis, the Wellington had a geodetically constructed airframe which enabled it to sustain massive battle damage and still keep flying. The 'Wimpey' bore the brunt of Bomber Command's night offensive until the arrival of the four-engined heavy bombers, the Short Stirling, Handley Page Halifax and Avro Lancaster.

Area bombing reached a climax in July-August 1943 when, in Operation Gomorrah, Bomber Command mounted a series of devastating raids on Hamburg. A subsequent attempt to 'wreck Berlin from end to end', which lasted from November 1943 to March 1944, was abandoned after losses of nearly 500 aircraft. However, German air defences were now becoming a wasting asset, while Bomber Command's range of Pathfinding and target-marking techniques was concentrating the maximum number of aircraft over the target in the minimum amount of time. By the end of the war Germany's cities lay in ruins.

Below: A magnificent view of the Merlin engines of the Avro Lancaster, Bomber Command's best heavy bomber. With a bombload of 14,000 pounds the Lancaster had a range of 1,660 miles. Specially adapted Lancasters carried the 22,000-pound Grand Slam bomb for use against hardened targets like U-boat pens and railway viaducts.

Below: A Lancaster overflies a blazing oil plant near Bordeaux during a daylight raid on 6 August 1944. Lancasters of Bomber Command flew 156,192 operational sorties during the war and dropped 608,612 tons of bombs on Germany; 3,345 Lancasters were reported missing.

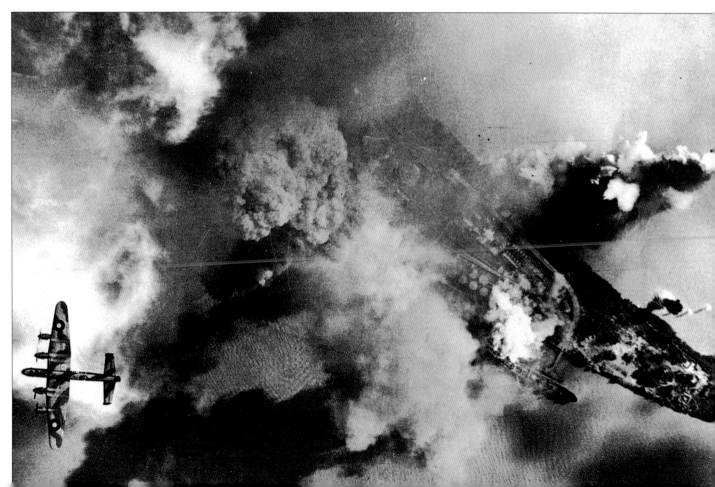

STRATEGIC BOMBING 2

WHILE THE RAF bombed Germany by night, the US Eighth Air Force, which arrived in England in the summer of 1942, bombed by day. US airmen arrived bristling with confidence that bombing would win the war.

At the core of the philosophy of the United States Army Air Force (USAAF) was the belief that high-level daylight precision bombing could destroy the key elements in the German war economy. The American bomber chiefs were convinced that, in the absence of a satisfactory long-range escort fighter, their bomber formations could fight their way to and from targets in Germany without suffering unacceptable losses. The Americans were not deterred by the fact that

Above: Boeing B-17 Flying Fortress bombers of US Eighth Air Force over Europe. Note the vapour trails of their fighter escorts. Maintaining formation required extreme concentration and physical effort from the B-17s' pilots. A 54-aircraft combat wing of 1943 was about 1.24 miles wide and half a mile deep, with 600 yards between the leading and trail aircraft in each of the wing's box-like 18-aircraft groups.

Left: A stricken B-17 of 94th Bombardment Group over Berlin, its tailplane mangled by bombs falling from aircraft flying higher in the formation. The 94th flew on the ill-fated Regensburg mission of 17 August 1943. Of 376 aircraft despatched on twin raids against war plants at Schweinfurt and Regensburg, 60 were lost and many more written off.

earlier in the war both Bomber Command and the Luftwaffe had employed these tactics and had failed.

In the skies over Germany the USAAF's theory was tested almost to the point of destruction. B-17 Flying Fortresses and B-24 Liberators, flying in mass formation, sustained increasingly heavy losses at the hands of the Luftwaffe's day fighters. By the late summer of 1943 average losses were running at 10 per cent per mission, a rate that could not be sustained, and morale had nosedived.

The crisis came to an end in December 1943 with the introduction of the formidable P-51 Mustang escort fighter, powered by a Rolls Royce Merlin engine and capable not only of escorting the bombers all the way to targets deep inside Germany but also of forming fighting patrols to sweep the skies clear of enemy fighters.

Right: Consolidated B-24 Liberators bomb Tours in France. Note the formation leader's smoke markers, which triggered simultaneous release of their bombs by the following aircraft to produce a pattern of bombs around the target. The Liberator and the Flying Fortress, both of which were heavily laden with defensive armament, could carry a 5,000-pound bombload over a range of about 2,000 miles.

Left: Suffer the little children. Refugees fleeing from the city of Dresden, in Saxony, which was destroyed in a series of raids delivered by Bomber Command and Eighth Air Force between 13 and 15 February 1945. The raids, in which up to 130,000 civilians perished, remain controversial today.

SIX MONTHS OF VICTORY

I N THE six months following Pearl Harbor, Japan cut a swathe through the Pacific, gaining vast territories for its 'Greater East Asia Co-Prosperity Sphere'. Faced with scattered, ill-equipped opposition, the Japanese secured victory with the brilliant use of intelligence, incisive central planning and the smooth co-ordination of naval, air and ground forces.

By May 1942 the territory in Japanese hands included the islands of Guam and Wake, the Philippines, French Indochina, Burma, Thailand, Malaya, Singapore, Hong Kong, the Dutch East Indies, three-quarters of New Guinea and Papua, the Bismarck Archipelago and a substantial part of the Gilbert and Solomon Islands. To the north, they threatened the Aleutian chain and the approaches to Alaska; in the west, having overrun Malaya, captured the great naval base at Singapore and bundled the

Below: Japanese landing parties storm ashore in the British colony of Hong Kong on 8 December 1941. Fighting continued until Christmas Day, when the British commander, Major-General C.M. Maltby, surrendered. The Japanese victory was followed by an orgy of killing and rape.

British out of Burma, they were close to the borders of India; to the south they menaced Australia.

The Japanese had reached the limits of conquest predicted by Admiral Yamamoto the C-in-C of the Japanese Combined Fleet. To secure their vast perimeter, they now sought to lure the US Pacific Fleet into battle and destroy it.

Above: Surrender in Singapore, 15 February 1941, the single most catastrophic defeat in British military history. Over 130,000 troops were taken prisoner.

Opposite: The doomed battleship *Prince of Wales*, which was sent to Singapore with the battlecruiser *Repulse* as the major units in Force Z. On 8 December 1941 *Prince of Wales* and *Repulse* sailed from Singapore to strike at Japanese transports supporting the landings in northern Malaya. Lacking air cover, they were sunk by Japanese level and torpedo-bombers on 10 December.

Right: Some of the 76,000 US and Filipino prisoners taken by the Japanese in the Bataan peninusla on Luzon in the Philippines. At least 20,000 of them died on the subsequent 'Death March' to their prison camp, a grim warning of the brutality meted out by the Japanese to Allied prisoners of war.

TURNING THE PACIFIC TIDE

AT THE Battle of the Coral Sea, 4-8 May 1942, the Japanese were halted and a new era in naval warfare was opened. The first large-scale aircraft carrier clash was fought without either surface fleet sighting the enemy.

At Coral Sea the Japanese sank one of Admiral Frank Fletcher's two carriers, *Lexington*, and damaged the other, *Yorktown*. Believing both carriers had been sunk, the Japanese fleet pressed on with its plan to capture the island of Midway. The Americans, who had cracked the Japanese naval code, positioned their fleet to defeat the much stronger task force which the Japanese had assembled to take Midway. In the ensuing carrier battle – one of the most decisive of the war – American dive-bombers destroyed four Japanese carriers and reversed the balance of power in the Pacific.

Below: A Douglas Dauntless dive-bomber over Wake Island. It was the Dauntless that did the most damage at Midway, either sinking or crippling four Japanese carriers. Underpowered, lacking range and exhausting to fly for any length of time, the Dauntless nevertheless managed to sink a greater tonnage of Japanese shipping than any other Allied aircraft.

Above: The US carrier *Enterprise* under attack at the Battle of Santa Cruz, 26 October 1942, an engagement during the battle for Guadalcanal which left the carrier *Hornet* a burning hulk, later sunk by the Japanese.

Above: Jungle conditions.
During the operations to isolate the Japanese base at Rabaul in December 1943 a tropical downpour drenches the crew of a 75mm gun as it fires on Japanese positions on New Britain in the Bismarck Archipelago.

The Japanese were now forced to defend a vast ocean empire which might be attacked at any point by the gathering might of the American war machine. The point the Americans chose was the Solomons chain. On 7 August 1942 US Marines stormed ashore on the island of Guadalcanal. The Japanese were not cleared from Guadalcanal until February 1943, after a series of savage ground, air and sea battles which stretched American endurance to the limit.

THE PROPAGANDA WAR

I N TOWNS and cities during the war years the pedestrian was
bombarded with exhortations to help the war effort in every
possible way. On a short walk, one Londoner counted 48
official posters on every subject from rationing to registering
for civil defence duties. In all the combatant nations these
posters were the visible symbols of the war effort.

The poster was the
principal instrument of
persuasion and expressed, in
the most direct terms, the
preoccupations of a nation's
leaders and the political,
military and moral
imperatives which drove
them, from simple appeals to
patriotism to the anti-
Semitism of Nazi ideology.
Radio, feature films and
newsreels also played their
part. Radio was used as a tool
of 'black propaganda' by all
sides, most famously by the
Germans in the person of
William Joyce, who broadcast
Nazi propaganda from
Hamburg and whose sneering
mock-aristocratic tones
earned him the derisive
nickname of 'Lord Haw Haw'.

Right: Bomb damage in the City of London fails to
disturb a banner bearing one of the most familiar
slogans of wartime Britain. In the drive to achieve
national self-sufficiency in food, golf courses were
turned over to the plough and small back gardens
came to resemble miniature farms, crammed with
chicken runs and rabbit hutches. The Albert
Memorial in Hyde Park was surrounded by
demonstration allotments.

Above: Josef Goebbels, the demon king of the propaganda war. After the defeat at Stalingrad, Goebbels became an increasingly important figure in the drive to achieve the total mobilization of the German war economy. On 24 August 1944 he was appointed Plenipotentiary for Total War with sweeping powers. Goebbels committed suicide, with his wife and children, in Hitler's Berlin bunker on 1 May 1945.

Right: A Nazi St George vanquishes a Jewish dragon.

In Josef Goebbels, Nazi Germany possessed a master of the art of propaganda, still capable of wrong-footing his Allied opponents at the end of the war. Intoxicated with his own skills, Goebbels nevertheless failed to grasp the simple fact that even the best propaganda was no match for the military might of the Allies. In April 1945, in the ruins of Berlin, Goebbels told his subordinates: *'. . . in a hundred years' time they will be making a fine colour film describing the terrible days we are living through. Do you not wish to play a part in that film?'*

THE MOVIES AT WAR

THE HOLLYWOOD film factory adapted to wartime production with the minimum of disruption. The war had cut the major studios off from many of their overseas markets. But there was a huge increase in cinema audiences at home. War workers had plenty of money to spend and craved escapist entertainment.

The US government quickly grasped the importance of film as propaganda. The familiar movie genres – crime thrillers, musicals and Westerns – were adapted to accommodate popular war themes. Patriotism proved immensely profitable for the big studios like MGM, Paramount and Warner Bros.

Below: A moment from *Fires Were Started* (1943), directed by Humphrey Jennings, a lyrical tribute to the work of the Auxiliary Fire Service during the London Blitz.

Below: David Niven in *The Way Ahead* (1944) which followed a band of recruits through their training and into battle in the Western Desert. Niven, who had been a peacetime Army officer before becoming a Hollywood star, also served with distinction in north-west Europe during the closing stages of the war.

In 1943 the number of films dealing either directly or indirectly with the war, reached a peak. As the war drew to a close, there was a growing demand for pure escapism in the form of musicals or costume dramas.

Wartime revived the flagging British film industry, which produced a steady stream of stirring documentaries about the 'People's War'. These had a strong influence on mainstream features. Movies like *Millions Like Us*, *The Way Ahead* and *Waterloo Road* focused their attentions on the lives of ordinary soldiers and civilians and brought a new feeling of realism to British cinema. In contrast, German wartime cinema consisted of a mixture of hymns to national history and military strength, anti-Semitic tracts and frothy escapism.

Right: Gordon Jackson and Patricia Roc in *Millions Like Us* (1943), an acutely observed populist drama set in an aircraft factory which drove home the message that the British were fighting a 'People's War'.

Left: Surrounded by admiring GIs of US Ninth Army, Marlene Dietrich tucks into a sandwich 'somewhere in Germany' in February 1945. Along with many Hollywood stars, Dietrich worked tirelessly to entertain the troops serving overseas, often near the front line.

HOLOCAUST

JEWS HAD been persecuted in Germany from the moment the Nazis came to power in 1933. In 1935 the Nuremberg Laws deprived them of full German citizenship. By November 1938 about 150,000 of Germany's 500,000 Jews had emigrated, although many found refuge in countries which were within the German Army's impending reach.

The diplomatic victories of 1938-9 brought many Eastern European Jews under Nazi control. The conquest of Poland and western Russia delivered millions more into Hitler's hands. On the orders of Heinrich Himmler, chief of the SS, massacres began almost immediately. Between June and November 1941, SS *Einsatzgruppen* (task groups) killed at least one million Jews behind German lines in Russia.

Below: A round-up of Jews in the Warsaw ghetto in 1943. The ghetto, which was sealed off from the rest of the city by a high wall, contained some 430,000 people riddled with disease and afflicted by starvation. In December 1941 it was estimated that over 200,000 people in the ghetto were without food or shelter. Corpses littered the streets covered with sheets of newspaper. From the summer of 1942 the Jews in the ghetto were systematically deported to the death camp at Treblinka 80 miles west of Warsaw.

Left: A German soldier watches a blazing building during the uprising in the Warsaw ghetto, April 1943. Young Jews had armed themselves to strike back at their tormentors. About 1,000 Jewish fighters, armed with rifles, pistols and home-made bombs fought a desperate battle for a month before they were overwhelmed by tanks, flamethrowers and aircraft. It was the last act in the history of the ghetto. Only about 100 Jews survived the uprising. The rest, some 60,0000, were killed in the fighting or sent to the death camps.

Most of the Jews were killed by mass shooting, a method Himmler considered inefficient. At the Wannsee conference in January 1942 he approved the 'Final Solution to the Jewish Problem'. Jews were rounded up in the ghettos to which they had been confined and sent to death camps in the East. Here they were either killed on arrival or worked to the point of death in SS factories before being consigned to the gas chambers. This was the fate which befell some six million Jews and many non-Jews as well, most of them forced labourers who were kept alive so long as they could work.

The removal of the Jews, if not their exact fate, was a fact known to everyone in Nazi-occupied Europe. From 1942 the Allied leadership was well aware of what was happening. But the saving of the Jews was not one of the Allies' war aims. It was not until the last months of the war, when the death camps were overrun, that the people of Britain and America were confronted with the terrible truth.

Right: A triumph of German civilization. The terrible remains of Hitler's 'New Order' at the Bergen-Belsen concentration camp, liberated by British troops on 15 April 1945. Many of the dead in this mass grave had succumbed to typhus, which had raged through the camp in the closing weeks of the war. When the British arrived they found 13,000 corpses lying in the open in grotesque piles.

THE ITALIAN CAMPAIGN

AFTER CLEARING North Africa, the Allies invaded Sicily on 9 July 1943. Led by Patton and Montgomery, US Seventh and British Eighth Armies fought with great dash but could not prevent most of the island's German defenders from disengaging and slipping across the straits of Messina to mainland Italy with the greater part of their equipment.

On 25 July, Mussolini was overthrown, and on 3 September an anti-fascist Italian government signed a secret armistice with the Allies. Six days later the Allies landed on the Italian mainland at Salerno, south of Naples.

Thereafter the Allied progress up the Italian peninsula was a long, hard slog, made all the more gruelling by difficult

Above: British troops of X Corps come ashore at Salerno, south-east of Naples, in September 1943, where they met stiff resistance from two German armoured divisions. Men and machines are being disgorged from a Landing Ship Tank (LST) designed to beach and fitted with opening bow doors.

Left: A soldier of 2nd New Zealand Division brings in two German prisoners under Castle Hill at Cassino, May 1944. The monastery which dominated the battlefield at Cassino was taken by the Polish II Corps after a savage battle. The four-month struggle for this vital link in the Gustav Line cost the Allies 21,000 casualties.

terrain, missed opportunities, stiff German resistance in a series of well-fortified defensive positions, notably the Gustav Line, and the constant drain on resources in the theatre by the priority given to the Normandy invasion. In January 1944 an amphibious landing at Anzio, behind the Gustav Line, briefly opened a window of opportunity but the chance was missed.

The strongpoint in the Gustav Line at Monte Cassino was taken in May 1944, after a bitter battle, and Rome fell on 4 June. But the Allies remained outnumbered by the German forces in Italy, and it was not until 29 April 1945 that the Germans surrendered. Far from proving the 'soft underbelly' of Churchill's imagining, Italy turned into a running sore in Allied strategy.

Right: General Mark Clark, commander of US Fifth Army, rides through St Peter's Square in Rome on 4 June 1944. The ambitious Clark frequently let his liking for personal publicity cloud his operational judgement.

THE WARLORDS

THE BROAD outlines of the war were determined by four men, Hitler, Stalin, Roosevelt and Churchill. The two dictators, Hitler and Stalin, displayed some striking similarities, adopting personal regimes which turned night into day – to the exhaustion of their staffs – and immersing themselves in the minutiae of operations, frequently with disastrous results.

As the war progressed Stalin reined in these tendencies and submitted to the advice of military professionals of the highest calibre, the battle-winner Zhukov and the staff officers Vasilevsky and Antonov. Nevertheless, he remained in total control from first to last, ruling his commanders by fear, as he did the Soviet Union.

Hitler assumed personal control of operations in December 1941, but it was a role for which he was not well suited. The easy victories of 1939 and 1940 had bred in him a contempt for his generals, the majority of whom had urged caution, and a corresponding reluctance to heed their practical advice. Sooner or later, those who stood up to him were dismissed. From 1943 Hitler fought the war from the map, clinging to a strategy of holding every inch of ground and leaving his best commanders little or no room for manoeuvre.

Above: Churchill, Roosevelt and Stalin meet for the last time at Yalta in the Crimea in February 1945, when the plans for the postwar divison of Germany were finalized. By then Roosevelt was a grievously sick man. He died of a brain haemmorrhage on 12 April. Churchill, who was to be ousted in the British general election of July 1945, was gloomily coming to terms with an exhausted Britain's reduced status at the top table. In contrast, Stalin emerged from the conference triumphant, having secured the Soviet Union's dominant position in Eastern Europe and substantial concessions from Roosevelt in return for the Soviet Union's entry into the war against Japan. The Soviet Union invaded Manchuria on 8 August 1945.

Right: Hitler and Mussolini in happier times in 1938. Although Mussolini was the senior dictator, having come to power in 1922, Italy was the junior partner in her alliance with Germany. From 10 June 1940, when Mussolini declared war on Britain and France, Italy proved a grave strategic embarrassment to Hitler. Mussolini was executed by Italian partisans on 28 April 1945.

Churchill also displayed an alarming tendency to meddle in operational matters, but most of his wildcat interventions were smoothly diverted by Field Marshal Brooke, the Chief of the Imperial General Staff, whose demanding task it was to translate his boss' strategic ambitions into hard reality, given Britain's stretched resources. The bond Churchill forged with President Roosevelt was crucial in co-ordinating Anglo-US strategy. In contrast to Churchill, however, Roosevelt remained aloof from the running of the war, retaining his peacetime routine after Pearl Harbor and leaving much in the hands of his immensely able Chief of Staff, General Marshall.

Left: The Japanese Emperor Hirohito reviews his troops in 1939. An ineffectual man, more interested in marine biology than military expansion, Hirohito exercised little influence over the senior commanders who determined policy until the closing stages of the war when defeat was inevitable. After the war he was not prosecuted as a war criminal, renounced his divine status and became one of the principal instruments of the American occupation of Japan.

OCCUPATION AND RESISTANCE

CONQUEST BRINGS its own problems: among them maintaining order in conquered territories, replacing governments and reviving and exploiting economies for the conquerors' profit.

The 'New Orders' established in Asia by the Japanese and in Europe by Germany reflected these concerns. Japanese rule in its Greater East Asia Co-Prosperity Sphere was harsh and often arbitrary but it was overshadowed by the cruelty of Germany's policy towards its conquered territories, driven as it was by Nazi racial policy. The victims were not only Jews or the millions of Russians forcibly transported to the Reich as slave labour. In Poland the German aim was not merely to dominate

Below: A German sentry stands guard on the Atlantic Wall, symbol of Hitler's 'Fortress Europe'.

but also to destroy the Polish national identity. The entire population were to become German slaves, forming a huge pool of cheap labour. In Greece, thousands starved when the Germans commandeered the food stocks.

In Occupied Europe, geography was one of the principal determinants of effective resistance. In the mountains of Yugoslavia, Marshal Tito's partisan army tied down large numbers of German and Italian divisions. In the Pripet marshes of Russia, thousands of guerrillas harassed the Wehrmacht. In small, flat Denmark, where the spirit of Resistance was strong, such operations were impossible.

Churchill hoped that in the West the Resistance, with British help, would *'set Europe ablaze'*. Ultimately, its effect was psychological rather than military, although during the Normandy invasion the French Resistance played a significant disruptive role behind German lines.

Below: Members of the French Resistance in action during the liberation of Paris, August 1944.

Opposite: A firing squad executes partisans in the Balkans. In December 1941 Hitler issued his 'Night and Fog' decree, whereby inhabitants of Occupied Europe who were deemed to 'endanger German security' but were not to be immediately executed, were to disappear into limbo. No news of their fate was to be released to their families. No one knows how many people were victims of this order.

Right: Legacy of occupation. Police lead a suspected collaborator away from a vengeful crowd in liberated Paris. In the immediate aftermath of liberation thousands of collaborators were summarily executed by the Resistance. Later thousands more were tried and sentenced to death or varying terms of imprisonment.

THE GERMAN HOME FRONT

ITLER'S WAR plans had envisaged a series of short, sharp campaigns. No preparations had been made to fight the 'Total War' which the British had embraced from 1940. Sweeping German victories in France and Russia spared most Germans many of the hardships of war. Goods of all kinds flooded in from the conquered territories. Until 1941 the peacetime routines of work, school and annual holidays were not disturbed.

German war industry marked time while the wives of soldiers away at the war lived comfortably off their state allowances. It was not until 1941 that any attempt was made to direct women into war factories. However, rationing and shortages began to bite in 1942 as Allied bombers brought German civilians into the front line and losses mounted on the Eastern Front.

Below: A German soldier lends a hand on the farm in 1943. Germans had experienced their first wartime food crisis in the winter of 1941-2, caused by lack of farm workers (called up for the attack on the Soviet Union) and freight cars (now used to supply the Eastern Front).

It was not until the beginning of 1943, when the tide was already turning against Germany, that Germany mobilized to fight 'Total War' under the overall direction of Josef Goebbels, Hitler's propaganda chief.

Even then the war economy remained a mass of contradictions, with six million workers still producing consumer goods and 1.5 million women employed as maids and cooks. Corruption and waste, bred by the warring Nazi Party fiefdoms encouraged by Hitler as a means of preserving his own authority, bedevilled the German home front to the end of the war. The whole system would have collapsed had it not been for the millions of slave workers transported to Germany from Eastern Europe.

Above: Ration cards are distributed to bombed-out civilians. The actress Hildegard Kneff, who grew up in wartime Berlin, remembered the diet of the mid-war years — weak ersatz coffee, margarine on rolls and 'powdered eggs, diluted and stirred, scrambled and fried and tasting of glue'.

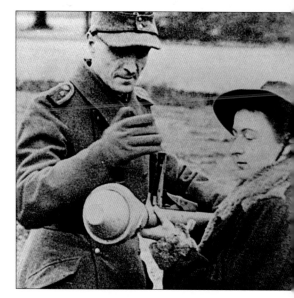

Above: A mobile kitchen provides a warming jug of soup for an air raid victim. From 1943 Allied bombers inflicted increasingly heavy damage on Germany's cities. Two-thirds of Hamburg's population were evacuated after the fire raids of August 1943; as the end of the war approached every third house in Berlin had been destroyed or rendered uninhabitable.

Right: Desperate measures. As the Russians close on Berlin a housewife receives instructions in the use of the Panzerfaust, a hand-held recoilless anti-tank weapon.

THE YANK INVASION

THE FIRST American troopship docked in Belfast on 26 January 1942, only seven weeks after the Japanese attack on Pearl Harbor. During the next three years nearly 1.5 million GIs – their equipment stamped 'GI' for General Issue – passed through Britain en route to Europe or to serve on bomber and fighter bases.

The Americans burst upon drab wartime Britain with all the brash vigour of a Technicolor Hollywood movie. One young woman recalled the arrival of American troops near Bournemouth: *'They swaggered, they boasted and they threw their money about, bringing a shot in the arm to business . . . and an enormous lift to the local female population.'*

They were not so popular with the local men, and British troops, who reflected that the Americans were *'overpaid, oversexed and over here'.* A US Army private drew ten shillings a day compared with the Tommy's two. GIs could afford to give girls a better time and

Below: GIs aquaint themselves with the British tea ceremony. Each GI had a little booklet, *A Short Guide to Britain*, the advice in which included: 'If you are invited to eat with a family, don't eat too much. Otherwise you might eat up their weekly rations. . . Don't try to tell the British that America won the last war or make wisecracks about the war debts or British defeats in this war'. For their part, the British welcomed the Americans, but were a little puzzled by the strict colour bar which operated in their armed forces.

shower them with cigarettes and nylons from their well-stocked PX stores. Small wonder that 'GI fever' swept Britain, from the American club at 'Rainbow Corner' in London's Piccadilly Circus to the smallest country hamlet. By D-Day 20,000 British women had become 'GI brides'. A less agreeable associated phenomenon was a soaring VD rate. By then, however, the Americans were moving on, into Europe, leaving many longing hearts behind.

Above: Men of an American armoured division are briefed before the D-Day landings. By June 1944 south-eastern and western England were so packed with men and material that the troops joked that if the invasion did not come soon, the island would sink.

Right: Hi, honey, you're home! US Marine Francis M. Connolly greets his British war bride Toni and their son Kenneth as they arrive with other GI brides in New York in February 1946.

THE RED ARMY ROLLS ON

BETWEEN DECEMBER 1943 and June 1944, a series of Soviet offensives drove the Germans out of the Crimea and the Ukraine and back into eastern Poland. While the struggle in Normandy in the days after D-Day absorbed Hitler and the Western Allies, the Red Army was gathering itself for a renewed attack.

Operation Bagration, named after Napoleon's Russian adversary in 1812, opened on 22 June, the third anniversary of Barbarossa. The offensive tore great holes in the front held by the German Army Group Centre. When the offensive finally ran down in August as it approached the River Vistula, it had punched a 250-mile gap in the German line, advanced 450 miles to the Gulf of Riga and the borders of East Prussia and destroyed the equivalent of 25 enemy divisions. The German Army Group Centre had been smashed and Army Group North isolated on the Baltic coast, where it was to remain, cut off, for the rest of the war. The German Army on the Eastern Front had been dealt a blow from which it would never recover.

Below: A massive column of German prisoners trudge wearily through the streets of Moscow. From Kursk (July 1943) to the final assault on Berlin the story on the Eastern Front was one of Russian advance and German retreat. The Red Army was to remain in undisputed possession of the initiative.

Bagration had brought the Red Army to the gates of Warsaw, where on 1 August 1944 the Polish Home Army rose up against the Germans. The Red Army did not come to the aid of the Poles but stood by while the Germans suppressed the uprising with great brutality. The Germans were not driven out of the Polish capital until January 1945.

Left: Soviet artillery, hammer of the German Army in the East. Drawing on a huge strategic reserve, the Red Army's artillery chief, Marshal Voronov, was able to mass crushing concentrations of guns in key sectors.

Below: T-34/85s in action with Marshal Malinovsky's Third Ukrainian Front west of Odessa in April 1944. In the Russian offensive of the first four months of 1944 the Red Army recovered the Ukraine and drove the Germans back to the Carpathians and almost to the borders of Poland.

Below: A salvo from a battery of Katyusha ('Little Kate') rocket launchers. A Red Army Katyusha division was capable of firing a barrage of 3,840 fin-stabilized rockets (230 tons of high explosive) up to a range of 3.5 miles. The Germans dubbed the Katyushas 'Stalin organs'.

OVERLORD

ANXIOUS TO deploy their massive resources, the Americans had urged the invasion of north-west Europe as early as the spring of 1943. The British, fearful of heavy losses, sought to postpone a landing until Allied air power had weakened the Germans.

In the summer of 1942 the British headed off an American plan for a 48-division invasion of northern Europe planned for April 1943. Thereafter, Britain and the US focused their immediate attention on clearing North Africa, and the invasion of Italy, which the British believed would draw troops away from France and pave the way for their planned cross-Channel invasion.

The Russians, suffering terrible casualties, wanted an immediate invasion – Stalin's 'second front'. In early 1943 Churchill and Roosevelt agreed to accelerate the build-up of US troops in Britain. However, to Stalin's displeasure, the operation was not to be launched before the middle of 1944.

The invasion of Normandy, codenamed *Overlord*, began on 6 June 1944. After a month-long air offensive and an Allied deception plan which convinced Hitler that the main attack would come in the Pas de Calais, where he held back a powerful armoured reserve, the largest amphibious operation in history got underway.

In the small hours of 6 June, Allied airborne troops landed to seize bridges and coastal batteries on the flanks of the invasion zone. The first Allied troops came ashore at 6.30pm. On only one of the five invasion beaches did the Germans mount fierce resistance. On Omaha Beach the US V Corps took heavy casualties from experienced and well-dug-in infantry. When they broke out of their beachhead on 'Bloody Omaha', V Corps left 2,400 dead behind them.

By midnight on 6 June 57,500 US and 75,000 British and Canadian troops had been landed. It took six weeks of hard fighting before the Allies were able to break out into Normandy and trap 50,000 retreating Germans in the Falaise pocket. Paris was liberated on 25 August 1944.

Opposite: Gliders litter the Normandy landscape after the airborne landings which preceded the assaults on the five target beaches. The parachute and glider-borne troops were scattered over wide stretches of country, many of them miles from their drop zones, but succeeded in sowing confusion among the German defenders of Normandy.

Above: Men of US V Corps come ashore at Omaha Beach, Normandy, on 6 June 1944. The fight for Omaha claimed 2,400 American lives. Private 'Buster' Hamlett of the 116th Infantry Division, who was wounded during the fighting, recalled the aftermath; 'As I painfully walked back to the beach, thousands of bodies were lying there. You could walk on the bodies, as far as you could see along the beach, without touching the ground'.

Right: An American infantryman and tank in the Normandy countryside, whose chequerboard of small fields, thick hedges and sunken lanes provided the perfect terrain for ambush.

Left: Men of the South Lancashire Regiment move up Sword Beach and on to capture strongpoints at Hermanville-sur-Mer, about half a mile inland. In the background the wounded receive first aid at the water's edge.

HITLER'S REVENGE WEAPONS

I N THE small hours of 13 June 1944 a small, pilotless aircraft with stubby wings chugged across the English Channel and plunged to earth about 25 miles from London. There was a huge explosion but no casualties. The first of Adolf Hitler's Vergeltungswaffen, or Revenge Weapons, had arrived in England.

Developed by the Luftwaffe, the V-1 (classified FZG-76 by the Germans) was cheap and easy to produce and was guided to its target by a gyroscopic automatic pilot. The Germans planned to bombard London with 500 V-1s each day. The flying-bomb was not particularly accurate, but London was a very big target. By the end of August 1944 approximately 21,000 people in the London region had been killed or seriously injured by the 'doodlebugs', as the V-1s were dubbed. A new wave of evacuation began. At night thousands sheltered in the Tube, as they had done during the Blitz.

By the autumn of 1944 the V-1-menace had been overcome by fast fighter aircraft, massed anti-aircraft batteries firing shells armed with proximity fuses and the capture by the Allies of the V-1 launching sites in northern France. Then, on 8 September, a new menace appeared — the V-2 rocket, developed by the German Army and designated the A-4.

The V-2 could not be shot down, nor did it give any warning of its approach, climbing to about 75 miles before hurtling to earth at four times the speed of sound. In all, 1,115 V-2s fell on England, 517 of them in the London area. Over 1,000 V-2s were also fired by the Germans at the port of Antwerp during the closing months of the war, to deny the Allies the use of its harbour.

On 27 March 1945 the last V-2 to reach England exploded in Kent. Two days later the last V-1 fell to earth about 20 miles from London. The V-weapons had caused extensive damage and killed nearly 9,000 people in Britain. They had given the British a nasty few months and had forced the Allies to devote considerable resources to deal with them. But none of this had halted the build-up of forces in Europe or broken civilian morale.

Below: A V-1 plunges to earth in central London. What made the V-1 particularly terrifying was the fact that it could be clearly heard approaching. When the doodlebug's guidance system told its motor to stop, there was 15 seconds' silence before it dropped out of the sky. If the engine cut out after the V-1 had flown overhead, you were safe. If not, the 15-second silence might be your last.

Left: Rescue teams at the site of a V-2 incident at London's Farringdon Market, 8 March 1945. Five days later a V-2 fell on Smithfield Market on a busy morning, killing 233 people.

Above: The V-2 rocket on its mobile launcher, which enabled it to be fired from almost any level piece of ground. The V-2 could carry a ton of explosives over a range of 200 miles. But each V-2 was at least 20 times more expensive for the Germans to produce than the V-1.

RACE TO THE RHINE

O N 15 August 1944 the Allies landed in the South of
France, capturing Toulon and Marseilles two weeks
later. In the north they raced into the Low Countries,
liberating Brussels on 3 September. On 11 September American
patrols crossed the German border near Aachen.

     Hopes that the war
would be over by Christmas
were soon dashed. A bold
airborne attempt to turn the
northern end of the West
Wall, the German defensive
line running along the Dutch
and French borders, came to
grief at Arnhem. The British
failed to clear the Scheldt
estuary, which denied Allied
shipping the use of the vital
port of Antwerp until
November 1944. In the great
forests on the German
frontier, the Reichswald and
the Hürtgen, there was
fighting reminiscent of the
slogging matches of the First
World War.

Above: A MkVI Tiger tank destroyed near Caen
during the breakout from the Normandy
bridgehead. The Tiger, introduced in 1942, was
ponderous in a fast-moving battle but heavily
protected and armed with the potent 88mm gun.
It often took at least half a dozen US M4 Sherman
medium tanks, the mainstay of British and
American armoured divisions, to knock out a
cornered Tiger.

Left: American anti-aircraft guns flank the
approaches to the railway bridge over the Rhine
at Remagen, which was seized by advanced units of
US First Army's 9th Armoured Division on 7 March
1945 after German engineers had failed to blow it.
The bridge collapsed into the river ten days later.

In December 1944 Hitler launched his last great offensive in the West. It fell in the Ardennes, the scene of his triumph in 1940, but this time he lacked the resources to engineer a second Dunkirk. In March 1945 the Allies closed up to the Rhine, and in a series of crossings broke into the heartland of the Reich, isolating the German Army Group B in the ruins of the industrial region of the Ruhr.

Right: Men of British 6th Airborne Division moving away from their Horsa gliders after landing east of the Rhine on 24 March 1945. The airborne landings were part of Operation Plunder, Field Marshal Montgomery's meticulously planned crossing of the Rhine at Wesel.

Below: The men of a defeated army. German prisoners taken by the British 21st Army Group in March 1945. In the West tens of thousands of German troops were surrendering *en masse*. In the East, they were preparing a last-ditch struggle against the Red Army, now readying itself for the final drive on Berlin, the 'Lair of the Fascist Beast'.

THE FORGOTTEN ARMY: THE BURMA CAMPAIGN

THE LOSS of Burma deprived the British of the use of the 'Burma Road', along which supplies had been passed to the Chinese generalissimo Chiang Kai-shek. His fight against the Japanese, however ineptly conducted, was the principal means of drawing enemy forces away from the war in the Pacific.

The first British attempt to regain access to the Burma Road was launched in the Arakan, the steamy coastal region of northern Burma on the Bay of Bengal, at the end of 1942. It was repulsed with almost contemptuous ease by the Japanese in March-May 1943. Nevertheless, morale was boosted by the success of an irregular operation mounted behind enemy lines by the Chindits, a deep-penetration force led by the brilliant, eccentric General Orde Wingate.

In December 1943 a second offensive was launched in the Arakan by British Fourteenth Army under the leadership of the highly capable General William Slim. It was supported by a second Chindit operation and an offensive in China directed by the American General Stilwell. However, in mid-March 1944 the Japanese Fifteenth Army went on the attack, threatening India with an invasion through the frontier posts of Imphal and Kohima.

In two epic battles for Imphal and Kohima the Japanese were decisively defeated and driven back to the River Chindwin, which Slim crossed in December 1944. He completed the destruction of Fifteenth Army at Meiktila in March 1945 and recaptured Rangoon, the Burmese capital, on 3 May. Burma had been reconquered and the Japanese withdrew in disorder towards Thailand.

Above: Japanese infantry present arms to the rising sun on the Indo-Burmese border. Allied troops had to learn to master the Japanese in their own element, the jungle, where the war was as much a battle against the jungle itself as the enemy. Casualties from malaria during the early part of the campaigns in Burma were far higher than those sustained in battle. Later the Allies profited from the use of antibiotics which were not available to their Japanese enemy.

Left: Jungle fighters. These 'Chindits' were members of long-range penetration groups formed by the then Brigadier Orde Wingate for air-supplied operations behind Japanese lines in Burma. Their name derives from their arm badge of a *chinthe* or stone lion which guards the entrance to Burmese temples. In the field the Chindits were divided into 300-strong self-supporting 'columns', each with its own mule train, heavy weapons and a signals detachment drawn from the RAF. The wounded Chindit in this photograph is lucky. Many wounded had to be left behind.

Below: Air power was vital to Allied victory in the Far East. Air drops sustained the Chindits and the defenders of Imphal and Kohima. Powerful fighters like these American Republic P47 Thunderbolts flown by the RAF were fitted with long-range tanks to enable them to strike deep into Burma to seek out air and ground targets. The Thunderbolt was a rugged aircraft with excellent speed and rate of roll. It could take a tremendous amount of damage and still bring its pilot home.

ARSENAL OF DEMOCRACY

THE WAR could not have been won without the massive material contribution made by American industry. The American genius for mass production was one of the Allies' most important weapons.

From March 1941 the United States supplied the British with weapons and war materials under the terms of the Lend-Lease Act. After the United States entered the war, the aid was extended to the Soviet Union. Over the next three years the United States provided its allies with civil and military aid sufficient for them to equip 2,000 infantry divisions. The key to victory in Europe and the Pacific lay in the sheer size and efficiency of the American economy, which applied the latest business methods to war production and the rapid expansion of the US armed forces.

In 1939 the United States manufactured only a small amount of military equipment for its own needs. By 1944 it was producing no less than 40 per cent of the world's armaments. In 1940 only 346 tanks had been built in the USA; in 1944 alone 17,500 rolled off the production lines. Figures for aircraft production leapt from 2,141 in 1940 to 96,318 in 1944.

Below: Liberty Ships nearing completion on the Pacific coast. Built as a mass-production riposte to the heavy loss of shipping in the Battle of the Atlantic, they were of simple, standardized construction, displacing 10,500 tons deadweight and driven by a single screw at a speed of 11 knots. By 1945 nearly 3,000 Liberty Ships had been built, seeing service in the Atlantic and Mediterranean and with the US Navy's massive fleet trains in the Pacific. Ironically, the basic design for these immensely useful craft had been produced by a shipping company in Sunderland, England, in 1879.

One wartime Ford plant employed 42,000 people. Much of their output was bound for the Soviet Union, which by 1945 had taken delivery of nearly 500,000 US-made trucks and jeeps. Red Army soldiers advanced on Berlin in American trucks or marched westwards in American boots, 15 million pairs of which went to the Soviet Union. Soviet war production was boosted by US machine tools, high-grade petroleum, steel, copper and rail locomotives and track. Shipping losses in the Battle of the Atlantic were offset by the construction of 3,000 Liberty Ships, general-purpose freighters whose average construction time was only 42 days. One Liberty Ship was built in just five days. The war years laid the foundation of American economic and industrial pre-eminence in the postwar era.

Left: A patriotic appeal to buy war bonds to safeguard the next generation. During the war the US economy surged ahead, with the gross national product rising by 60 per cent, providing most Americans with unparalleled prosperity.

Below: Women at work on the fuselage of the B-29 Superfortress bomber in the Boeing plant at Seattle on the Pacific coast. Women found new opportunities in the aircraft plants, where they often made up over 50 per cent of the workforce. The net effect was to bring a permanent increase in the proportion of women in the labour force.

THE INTELLIGENCE WAR

O NE OF the greatest Allied technical triumphs of the war was won, not on the battlefield, but in the English countryside at Bletchley Park, the home of the British Government Code and Cypher School.

It was here that the British deciphered the top-secret German signals encoded on their Enigma machines, one of which had found its way into British hands in 1939. British radio interception networks listened to the apparently meaningless groups of letters encoded by Enigma and transmitted in Morse code. They were taken down and sent to Bletchley, where the secret of Enigma was unlocked by matching electro-mechanical computers to the electric wiring of the Enigma machine. In this way British decoders discovered the Enigma keys, the settings that were changed three times a day. Eventually many Enigma signals were being read at the same speed by the British as the Germans.

Right: General Heinz Guderian, commander of XIX Panzer Corps, in his armoured command vehicle in France in 1940. In the foreground is a German Enigma code machine with its typewriter keyboard. Inside the machine was a complex system of gears, electric wiring and a series of drums. Each of the drums carried an alphabet on the outside. Any letter typed on the Enigma keyboard could be transposed into an infinite variety of different letters by the drums inside. The Germans were convinced that Enigma's coded messages, from which no apparent pattern could be discerned, were unbreakable.

Information from the deciphered Enigma signals was codenamed Ultra. It ranged from routine orders to detailed battle plans. Ultra was surrounded by the greatest secrecy to prevent the Germans discovering that the code had been broken. The British shared Ultra with the Americans but only provided their Soviet allies with summaries of Ultra-derived information. But there was at least one Soviet spy at Bletchley. This was John Cairncross, who provided Soviet intelligence with a detailed picture of Ultra. To the end of the war, the Germans never realized that the supposedly unbreakable Enigma code had been cracked.

Below: The Japanese carrier *Hiryu* ablaze at the Battle of Midway, June 1942. Long before Japan had entered the war, US Navy codebreakers had broken its naval and diplomatic codes. Information from these codes, distributed under the codename Magic, played a key role in American victory at Midway.

Below: Admiral Yamamoto (right), commander of the Japanese Combined Fleet. In April 1943 intercepted and decoded Japanese signals enabled American fighters to intercept and shoot down Yamamoto while he was on a tour of inspection in the western Pacific.

THE COMMANDERS

THE WAR threw up many military leaders with markedly different command styles. Their strengths and weaknesses continue to be debated and dissected by military historians and will provide a source of controversy for years to come.

For the Western Allies it was essential that the top positions were occupied by men who were diplomats as well as soldiers. These qualities were combined in the person of the American General Dwight D. Eisenhower, the Supreme Commander Allied Forces Europe from December 1943. 'Ike' was no fighting general but his emollient qualities held together a coalition in which temperamental subordinates like Patton and Montgomery sometimes seemed to be more at war with each other than the enemy.

Below: General Dwight D. Eisenhower with men of the US 101st Airborne Division a few hours before the launching of the invasion of Normandy. Eisenhower remains the epitome the managerial commander.

Both Patton and Montgomery were anything but diplomatic, but they inspired enormous confidence in their troops, as did Monty's brilliant opponent Rommel, the 'Desert Fox', one of the few genuinely romantic figures of the war and a general who liked to lead from the front, as did the armoured expert Guderian. On the German side, however, the outstanding operational commander was, without doubt, von Manstein, the man responsible for Hitler's decision to strike through the Ardennes in 1940 and the Red Army's most formidable enemy on the Eastern Front, where he was the master of the crushing counterstroke against a Russian breakthrough.

Three commanders stand out from the rest: the Japanese Yamamoto, the American MacArthur and the Russian Zhukov. Admiral Yamamoto was the mastermind behind the attack on Pearl Harbor who had the foresight to guarantee the Emperor Hirohito only six months of victory. General Douglas MacArthur's wartime career began with the loss of the Philippines, from which he recovered to display a masterly grasp of the possibilities of combined operations in the Pacific. Vain, tactless and domineering, MacArthur was nonetheless a commander of tactical skill and strategic vision. The third of the great commanders was Marshal of the Soviet Union Georgi Zhukov, who for much of the war, as Deputy Supreme Commander-in-Chief, was second only to Stalin in military affairs. Zhukov was Stalin's battle-winner: at Moscow in December 1941; at Stalingrad a year later; at Kursk in the summer of 1943 and thence all the way to the battle for Berlin in April 1945.

Above: Field Marshal Erwin Rommel, a charismatic figure who met a tragic end. Suspected of complicity in the attempt to assassinate Hitler at his East Prussian headquarters on 20 July 1944, Rommel was offered the choice between taking poison and a show trial. Rommel chose the poison and was buried with full military honours.

Below: Marshal Zhukov on the steps of the Reichstag after the fall of Berlin. Although by Soviet standards Zhukov was economical with the lives of the millions of men under his command, he nevertheless brought a ruthlessness to the battlefield which would have been unacceptable to the Western Allies.

Left: Master of amphibious warfare. General Douglas MacArthur with his trademark corncob pipe and, as usual, plenty of cameramen in attendance.

Opposite: General (later Field Marshal) Montgomery at El Alamein in his Grant command tank. Montgomery's flair for publicity was coupled with an immensely painstaking approach to the waging of war and insistence on the accumulation of maximum strength before the opening of an attack. Frequently criticized for over-caution, he was nevertheless the British Army's supreme battle-winner.

ASSAULT ON BERLIN

O N 12 January 1945 the Red Army burst out of its bridgeheads on the Vistula and drove to the line of the Oder, bringing Zhukov's First Belorussian Front to within 50 miles of Berlin. Fleeing before the Red Army onslaught was a tidal wave of ethnic German refugees, driven from their homes in the East.

Hitler had declared Berlin a fortress, but it was a stronghold which existed only in his imagination, defended by shattered formations and the boys and old men of the German Home Guard, the Volkssturm.

On 16 April, after massive preparations, Stalin launched his final drive on Berlin, secure in the knowledge that the British and Americans had abandoned the race to seize the German capital. By 27 April Berlin's defenders had been squeezed into a narrow east-west corridor about three miles wide and twelve miles long.

The city was cut off from the outside world. Russian shells plunged down on the city centre, shaking the underground bunker in which Hitler had taken refuge. On 30 April the Führer committed suicide in the bunker. On the afternoon of 2 May General Weidling, the commander of what was left of Berlin's garrison, surrendered to the Red Army. A general surrender of German forces followed on 7 May, at Eisenhower's HQ at Rheims, and on 8 May to Zhukov in Berlin.

Left: Russian armour rolls into Berlin. In taking the city the Red Army lost nearly 305,000 men killed wounded and missing, the heaviest casualties it suffered in any battle during the war. At least 100,000 German soldiers and civilians died in the battle.

Above: The Red flag flies over the Reichstag, which fell to the Russians on 30 April 1945. Only 200 yards away Hitler and his mistress Eva Braun had committed suicide in the Führerbunker. On 25 April US and Russian troops had met at Torgan on the Elbe.

Left: Last-ditch defenders of the Reich. Men of the Berlin Volkssturm, many of them armed with Panzerfausts, are mustered in December 1944. All males between the ages of 16 and 60 who were not in the armed forces but were capable of bearing arms were liable for service in the Volkssturm.

Right: The boy defenders of the Third Reich. Members of the Hitler Youth captured by the Russians during the Battle of Berlin.

VE-DAY

BY THE spring of 1945 the end of the war seemed to have been a very long time coming. With the announcement of Hitler's death, expectations of victory in the West were raised to fever pitch, but still people were kept waiting.

The reason was an agreement between the the Allies not to announce that peace had broken out until the Germans had signed instruments of surrender in Rheims and Berlin. A tight control was kept on the journalists in Rheims, but this did not prevent an enterprising Associated Press man breaking the story. News of the German surrender reached New York on 7 May. Eisenhower, the Supreme Allied Commander, was mad but the population of the Big Apple went berserk. That night, on British radio, it was announced that 8 May would be Victory in Europe Day and a public holiday.

Below: Queen Elizabeth, King George VI and Winston Churchill, flanked by Princess Elizabeth and Princess Margaret, make one of their many VE-Day appearances on the balcony at Buckingham Palace.

In Britain, street parties and bonfires, both long in preparation, were the principal features of the VE-Day celebrations. Hitler went up in smoke on many a suburban funeral pyre, the flames kindling memories of the Blitz. The lights that blazed in towns and cities that night alarmed many small children who had grown up with the blackout.

The joy was tinged with the sadness caused by the loss of loved ones in six years of conflict, and the awareness that there was a still a war to be won in the Far East.

Left: Crowds swarm over a truck in central London during the VE-Day celebrations. The British were jubilant but would soon be feeling the effects of 'the morning after'. Britain had virtually bankrupted herself fighting the war and in the words of the economist John Maynard Keynes was facing a 'financial Dunkirk'.

Right: While Europe rejoices at the end of of an evil tyranny, two elderly Berliners contemplate the ruins of the Third Reich.

ACROSS THE PACIFIC

AFTER THE clearing of Guadalcanal the Allied Pacific drive leapfrogged towards Japan in a strategy dubbed 'island hopping'. One by one the island stepping stones across the ocean were seized by Allied forces while the major Japanese bases were isolated and left to 'wither on the vine'. The final attacks on the Japanese home islands were to be launched from the Philippines through Okinawa, from the Marianas through Iwo Jima, and from the Aleutians.

The US Marine Corps, which was in the forefront of these amphibious operations, encountered fanatical resistance. On the atoll of Tarawa, taken after bitter fighting in

November 1943, only 146 Japanese surrendered out of a garrison of nearly 5,000 men. In February-March 1945 the capture of Iwo Jima, an island a mere eight miles square, claimed nearly 7,000 American lives and left 19,000 wounded. A similar number of US troops died in the fight for Okinawa, the scene of one of the grimmest battles of the Pacific war, in which 110,00 Japanese soldiers and 150,000 civilians died, many of them preferring suicide to capture.

Above: US Marines race across open ground at Tarawa, November 1943. Tarawa was surrounded by a high reef on which many landing craft ran aground, leaving men a long wade ashore under murderous fire. Learning from the losses at Tarawa, the Marine Corps stepped up the production of amphibious tracked vehicles (amtracs), capable of powering ashore and across heavily defended beaches before disembarking the troops they carried.

The Pacific drive provoked a series of furious naval battles in which the Japanese Navy was broken on the anvil of American air power. By mid-1944 all 15 of the Japanese carriers brought into service since 1941 had been sunk or put out of action by the US Navy.

Right: US Marines hug the black sand of Iwo Jima, scene of one of the grimmest battles in the Pacific war. Iwo Jima was less than two hours' flying time to Japan, making it a key objective in the drive towards the Japanese home islands. The island, dominated by Mount Suribachi, which rises behind the men in on the beach, was heavily fortified and defended to the death by a garrison of 22,000 Japanese troops of whom only 212 chose to surrender.

Below: Amtracs churn towards Okinawa, 1 April 1945, while the 16-inch guns of a US battleship plaster the shoreline. In taking the island the Americans ground forces suffered their heaviest casualties of the Pacific war, including 7,500 dead. Over 5,000 US Navy personnel died in kamikaze suicide attacks on their ships, 38 of which were sunk.

THE DESTRUCTION OF JAPAN

FOR SOME time the islands of Japan remained beyond the range of land-based American bombers. But the capture of the Mariana Islands in June-August 1944 gave the USAAF a springboard from which to launch its B-29 heavy bombers against Japan's cities.

Below: A Japanese aircraft falls blazing from the sky during the fight for the Marianas in June 1944.

From November 1944 the B-29s of 21st Bomber Command had concentrated on precision attacks on Japanese war industry, achieving only limited success. At the beginning of 1945 the emphasis was switched to a general urban bombing offensive aimed at demoralizing the population and exploiting the particular vulnerability of the close-packed Japanese cities to incendiary raids.

The match was put to the Tokyo tinder box on the night of 9/10 March 1945 when nearly 300 B-29s launched a devastating fire

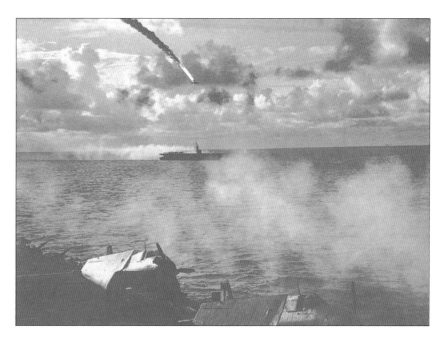

Left: Boeing B-29 Superfortress bombers over Yokohama on 29 May 1945. Introduced to combat in 1944, the B-29 was used exclusively in the Pacific. Its advanced technology included pressurization in the nose and parts of the fuselage and remote-controlled gun turrets. Cruising at 220mph at a height of 30,000ft, the B-29 could carry 5,000 pounds of bombs over a range of 1,600 miles or a maximum payload of 20,000 pounds over short ranges. While the bombers levelled Japan's cities, US submarines tightened the grip on Japan by sinking the shipping on which Japanese war industry depended for its oil and raw materials.

raid which destroyed over 250,000 buildings, killed at least 100,000 people and drove another million into the countryside. Operating with almost complete freedom, 21st Bomber Command levelled city after city. By the end of June, approximately half of the built-up areas of Tokyo, Nagoya, Osaka, Kawasaki, Kobe and Yokohama had been consumed by firestorms. Coastal shipping movements were halted as American bombers sowed thousands of acoustic and magnetic mines in the waters around the Japanese home islands. By the end of July there were virtually no targets left.

Opposite: Carriers and aircraft, the foundation of American air power in the Pacific. Curtiss SB2C Helldiver bombers return to the carrier *Hornet* after a strike against Japanese shipping in the China Sea, January 1945. The powerful Helldiver was a difficult aircraft to fly and never popular with aircrew, who nicknamed it 'Son of a Bitch, Second Class'.

Right: The flight deck of the US carrier *Bunker Hill* after direct hits by two kamikaze aircraft within the space of one minute on 11 May 1945 during the battle for Okinawa.

BUILDING THE A-BOMB

AT DAWN on 16 July 1945 a colossal fireball burst over the New Mexico Desert, fusing the sand to glass and exploding with a force equivalent to 20,000 tons of TNT. A huge mushroom cloud boiled thousands of feet into the sky. With the testing of the first atomic bomb, a new era in warfare had dawned.

After the attack on Pearl Harbor, many of the Allies' most brilliant scientific brains were gathered together in a specially built laboratory complex at Los Alamos in New Mexico. By 1945 about 125,000 people were engaged on the top-secret Manhattan Project to build an atomic bomb. It was only after the war that Allied scientific teams investigating Germany's atomic weapons programme discovered that German research into nuclear weapons lagged behind the Allies by at least two years. Hitler's bomb remained a fantasy.

Only in America could the massive resources necessary to develop the bomb be concentrated. The eventual cost was some two billion dollars. Three weeks after the desert test, the bomb was used against Japan. President Roosevelt's successor, Harry S. Truman, had been advised that an invasion of mainland Japan would cost up to a million casualties. To bring a speedy end to the war in the Pacific, and to provide a demonstration of US military power to the Soviet Union, Truman sanctioned the use of the bomb against Japanese cities.

On 6 August an American B-29 heavy bomber dropped a
Uranium-235 version of the bomb, the torpedo-shaped 'Little
Boy' on the city of Hiroshima, killing 78,000 people. On 9 August
another B-29 dropped 'Fat Man', a bulbous plutonium bomb,
on Nagasaki, where 35,000 died. Japan formally surrendered to
the Allies on 2 September.

Opposite: The man who delivered the bomb,
Colonel Paul Tibbets, the leader of Crew 15, whose
men trained to drop the atomic bombs on Japan.
On 6 August 1945 he piloted his B-29, named
'Enola Gay' after his mother, to Hiroshima,
releasing the six-ton 'Little Boy' nuclear device
from a height of 31,600 feet. The destructive
power of the bomb was equal to the bombload
of nearly 2,000 B-29s carrying conventional
high-explosive.

Opposite: Ground zero. The ruins of Hiroshima a
few days after the A-bomb attack. Over 100,000
Japanese were killed by the bombs dropped on
Hiroshima and Nagasaki. Later, thousands more
died of radiation sickness.

Above Left: A victim of the atomic bomb in a
makeshift hospital in Hiroshima. The scars of the
city of Hiroshima may now have healed but not
the physical scars suffered by survivors who were
exposed to the full blast of the bomb.

Above: A mushroom cloud rises to 20,000 feet over
Nagasaki after the explosion of the second atomic
bomb on 9 August 1945.

AFTERMATH

I N THE late summer of 1945 the world was exhausted by war. The cities of Germany and Japan had been levelled by Allied bombers. In Japan, Hiroshima and Nagasaki had been destroyed by atomic bombs.

Huge areas of Europe and Southeast Asia had been devastated by the fighting. Road, rail and canal systems had been destroyed. Ports were choked with wreckage. In Europe a severe drought followed by a disastrous harvest threatened famine in the worst-hit areas. In the western Soviet Union 25 million people were homeless.

In Europe the future looked bleak. The wartime alliance between the United States, Britain and the Soviet Union was fast breaking up. Europe was being divided into two separate and hostile camps: one in Eastern Europe already dominated by the Soviet Union, the other in Western Europe soon to be rescued from political and economic collapse by the United States. The forward flash point of a new conflict, the Cold War, was a divided Germany and its former capital, Berlin, lying deep in the Soviet zone of occupation.

The European nations which had gone to war in 1939 did not dictate the terms of peace. The Allied strategic aims of the later war years, and the shape of the postwar world, were determined at the great wartime conference by two non-European powers, the United States and the Soviet Union. Soviet hegemony was established in Eastern Europe. In 1945 Poland, the country for which the British and French had gone to war in 1939, exchanged occupation by the Nazis for a long Soviet tyranny.

Below: Captured Nazi standards are tossed on to a pile outside Lenin's tomb in Moscow's Red Square.

In the Pacific the defeat of Japan ensured American domination of the region. The humiliation which the Japanese had inflicted on the colonial powers in the Far East in 1941-2 meant that the empires which the latter had shed so much blood and treasure to regain would soon be threatened by a tide of nationalism.

Below: The defendants in the dock at the war crimes trial which began in Nuremberg in November 1945. On the left is the bulky figure of Hermann Göring. next to him, with arms folded, is Rudolf Hess, Hitler's former deputy, who was ignored by his co-defendants throughout the trial. On Hess' left are Ribbentrop, formerly the German foreign minister and Field Marshal Keitel, chief of staff of the German Army.

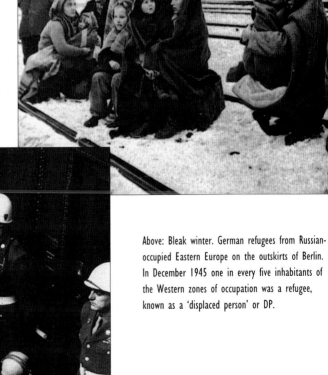

Above: Bleak winter. German refugees from Russian-occupied Eastern Europe on the outskirts of Berlin. In December 1945 one in every five inhabitants of the Western zones of occupation was a refugee, known as a 'displaced person' or DP.

COUNTING THE COST

I T IS estimated that some 64 million people died as a result of the Second World War, 24 million soldiers and 40 million civilians. The Soviet Union suffered the most grievous losses, with 8.6 million soldiers dead or missing and nearly 8 million civilians killed. Recent figures which have emerged from Russian archives suggest this figure may have to be revised upwards. Most of the Soviet civilians, the majority of them Ukrainians and White Russians, died as a result of deprivation, reprisal and forced labour. In relative terms, Poland suffered the worst of all the combatant countries. About eight million people – one in four of the population – had died. The death toll in the Polish capital, Warsaw, was higher than the combined wartime casualties of Britain and the United States.

In Yugoslavia civil and guerrilla war killed at least a million. The number of casualties, military and civilian, in Eastern Europe was swollen by the ferocity of the war waged in this theatre and the German racial oppression of Jews and Slavs. Nevertheless, casualties were bad enough in France, Italy and the Netherlands. Before June 1940 and after November 1942 the French army lost 200,000 dead; 400,000 French civilians died in air raids or concentration camps. Italian losses were 330,000, half of them civilians. In Holland 200,000 – all but 10,000 of them civilians – died as a result of bombing or deportation. Their oppressor, Germany, lost 3.5 million military personnel dead or missing and 2 million civilians. The Western Allies did not suffer such horrific losses, but the price of victory was high. The British armed forces lost 244,000 men and their Commonwealth and imperial allies another 100,000. Some 60,000 British civilians died as a result of bombing by the Luftwaffe and the V-weapons. In the United States there were no civilian casualties of war. American military losses were 292,000 dead or missing. In contrast, the Japanese lost 1.2 million men in battle. Nearly a million Japanese civilians died in the war.

Below: Allied casualties after the abortive cross-channel Dieppe raid of 19 August 1942. The operation, codenamed Jubilee, was intended to soothe Soviet anxiety about the lack of a 'second front' in Europe, but resulted in heavy loss of life. Although the raid remains controversial, it provided Allied planners with much information which was put to good use in the preparation and execution of the Normandy landings in June 1944.